THE STORY OF
HALTON HOUSE

by
Squadron Leader Beryl E Escott BA ARDS MBIM WRAF

Foreword by
Squadron Leader M J W Bourton RAF

FOREWORD

The history of Halton House is an evolutionary history and not one that has stood still as has become the case of many of the nation's country houses. The remarkable story of this house spans from the late 19th century until the present and I am sure there is more to come. The building may now creak and groan but when the music floats across the gardens on the night of the Summer Ball the whole era of the Victorian Rothschilds is brought back to life.

This third edition of 'The Story of Halton House' has remained essentially true to the original but has included colour plates for the first time, to complement the descriptive lines of the author, Squadron Leader Beryl Escott. As one of a long line of Halton House Historians it has been a privilege to be a small part in preserving the story of this fascinating house. Together with my fellow historian, Flight Lieutenant Julia Trasler, we will continue to work towards that end until the time comes to pass on the mantle. I have great faith that future generations will also benefit from this story and may even have the chance, as I have had, to live within its four walls.

I trust you will find this story both interesting and revealing as you turn the pages and delve deep into the life of Alfred de Rothschild.

Squadron Leader Michael Bourton

© Halton House Officers' Mess 2003
3rd Edition
ISBN 0-9540 312-1-0

THE STORY OF
HALTON HOUSE

INTRODUCTION

"History is the essence of innumerable biographies" - Carlyle

Halton House as you see it today came to the Royal Air Force just after the First World War and has been used as an Officers' Mess ever since. It is only about a century old and was the brainchild of one owner, a member of the Banking family of Rothschild.

This account endeavours to convey the story and the flavour of the Mansion itself. Inevitably it also deals with the life of its creator Alfred de Rothschild. His passing marked the end of an era.

In the aftermath of World War One, the face of rural England radically altered and the function and ownership of the house underwent a complete change. These events highlight, even more clearly, the contrast of Halton House as it is today, with its image as a great country house in its Victorian and Edwardian prime.

4   **Chapter 1**
A HOUSE PARTY AT HALTON

12   **Chapter 2**
ALFRED'S FAMILY

24   **Chapter 3**
THE ROTHSCHILDS IN THE VALE OF AYLESBURY

30   **Chapter 4**
ALFRED BUILDS

38   **Chapter 5**
HALTON ESTATE

48   **Chapter 6**
FIRST VISITORS

CONTENTS

54   **Chapter 7**
THE SERVICE WING

66   **Chapter 8**
THE MAIN HOUSE

96   **Chapter 9**
THE GARDENS

104   **Chapter 10**
BEFORE THE GREAT WAR

108   **Chapter 11**
THE ROYAL AIR FORCE TAKES
OVER

114   **HALTON HOUSE PAINTINGS**

118   **THE LAST WILL**

125   **ACKNOWLEDGEMENTS (Third Edition)**

126   **INDEX**

CHAPTER 1

Alfred de Rothschild

A HOUSE PARTY

AT HALTON

"On with the dance! Let joy be unconfined! No sleep till morn when youth and pleasure meet to chase the glowing hours with flying feet." Byron

Sitting at his desk in the picture-lined room of his elegant London home, Alfred Charles de Rothschild writes in his sprawling hand, with many flourishes, his gilt edged invitations to a Weekend House Party at Halton. Duly delivered next day, by the famous dark blue Rothschild cabs, the acceptances soon start flowing in. Now Alfred looks forward eagerly to a holiday in his country retreat with some interesting and interested friends.

Never up early any morning, Alfred usually takes the day off from the Bank on a Friday. Instead, a courier delivers £1,000 in crisp new banknotes and gold sovereigns to his home at Seamore Place. Here, last minute arrangements are made, a few early guests arrive and at length, accompanied by his gigantic valet and mountains of luggage, Alfred is solicitously installed with his friends in his carriage, with its mink footwarmer and other luxuries, to travel to the station where they will join his own special coach on the Aylesbury train. What matter if Alfred is slightly late, the guard knows better than to let the train depart without its distinguished patron. Once aboard, the train has a swift and untroubled journey down the line to Wendover or Tring station, other local trains being shunted aside while the steam engine, pulling the unmistakable blue and yellow Rothschild coach, runs smoothly through.

Messages crackle over the telegraph wires so that when Alfred arrives at the station, transport awaits to take him and his guests the rest of the journey to his house. In the early days, these would be barouches drawn by matched horses, beautifully caparisoned with harness of tooled leather and gold, the drivers' whips being embellished with a large blue bow. In later years carriages would be replaced by one of his 'famous five' fleet of cars often with one following discreetly in the distance as insurance against breakdown.

His arrival causes a stir in the villages of Tring or Wendover, which suddenly burst into activity. There is much coming and going down the cobbled streets. Visitors mean trade and Alfred means trade on a generous scale and local shop keepers and businesses are not slow to seize their advantages. At Wendover's Red Lion Hotel, convivial customers are warned to take extra care as they leave the archway onto the busy High Street, while members of Alfred's private orchestra jostle shoulder to shoulder with some of the overflow from the house party in search of accommodation at the Shoulder of Mutton and other local hostelries.

HIS ARRIVAL CAUSES A STIR IN THE VILLAGES OF TRING OR WENDOVER, WHICH SUDDENLY BURST INTO ACTIVITY. THERE IS MUCH COMING AND GOING DOWN THE COBBLED STREETS.

Kitchener of Khartoum

Folk hurry out to bow or curtsey as Alfred's carriage bowls by, this deference being particularly marked in the neat, bright, little village of Halton. At the mansion, after completing the circuit around the drive, the carriage comes to a stop under the porch in winter or at the terrace steps behind the house in summer. Here the staff stands in stately line, while the carriage steps are unfolded and the master alights, himself helping down any distinguished ladies in his company.

Their coats and hats whisked away, guests are politely ushered into the salon and asked to add their names to the visitors' book - a most varied one, bearing the signatures of royalty, statesmen, diplomats, politicians, actresses, society beauties and musicians. In it can be seen such names as Kitchener of Khartoum, Disraeli, Lily Langtry, the Shah of Persia, Liszt, Mr Asquith, Lord Carnarvon and the Prince of Wales. This duty completed the housekeeper steps forward and guests are escorted to their dressing rooms on the balcony, loud in praise of the rooms and the furnishings around them. Even more delighted are their reactions when, with doors opened, they discover their rooms ablaze with coloured draperies and vases of rare flowers, little baskets of rare greenhouse fruit and decorative boxes of tempting little chocolates or pralines.

Lily Langtry

A specially-made fresh spray or buttoniere - beads of moisture still hanging from its petals - is reflected twice over in the dressing-table mirror. Beside the secondary stairs the lift is hard at work transporting trunks and boxes from the luggage entrance to the bedrooms, so that guests often find their maids or valets already unpacking and laying out their evening clothes. Everything at Halton House is the last word in luxury and efficiency even to the bath, already being filled, scented with favourite perfumes or herbs for the tired occupant to rest and relax after the rigours of the journey.

Having arranged for his weekend spending money to be lodged in the great safe with its household silver and plate, Alfred, however, lingers behind. He still has further guests to welcome. For a short time he adjourns to his business room, where he can stand in front of his paintings, taking refreshment from their beauty, and perhaps ask himself for the umpteenth time, why, now he is here, he doesn't stay for good instead of rushing back to the hurly burly of London. Thoughtfully, he sniffs at the red carnation in his buttonhole. Even without telephone or telegraph, messages will be relayed at night by lamps and in the day by outriders, to warn him of the imminent arrival of more of his guests. From his window he can see them arrive and be at the door to welcome them as they step down. Then the same ceremony and solicitous care before they too join the others in their rooms upstairs.

Soon the house is full, corridors echo with hurrying feet. Through an opening door comes the chatter of voices, laughter, water swishing - a servant stands back and bobs while one guest passes in search of a friend - greetings, the rumble of conversation, the door closes. Alfred slowly ascends the grand staircase, dogged anxiously by his valet. He is pleased but weary. Everyone has arrived. Everything is in order. Now for a short rest in his red dressing room, some tea and perhaps a nap before the serious business of the evening begins.

Early this evening Alfred stands in the Drawing Room welcoming his guests.

The ladies wear full evening dress, low necks, lace and satin bustles, short trains and jewels in their hair. Queen Victoria would not have been amused.

"One of the new fashions of our very elegant society is to go in perfectly light-coloured dresses, without a particle of a shawl or scarf (as I was always accustomed to wear and see others wear)."

The gentlemen wear white ties and waistcoats, black tailcoats and no decorations - unless Royalty was present - all identical in black and white, like stately penguins.

Alfred demurely accepts their compliments and suggests a conducted tour of his art collection until the time for dinner. This could take many hours, were it not that, ever considerate of his guests, Alfred suggests a short adjournment in the winter garden to take a water ice or a glass of wine. Then back to the paintings, the tapestries, the vases, the sculpture.

"Sèvres everywhere" gasps an awed lady. Her escort whispers, "Some say the ornaments on a single mantlepiece are worth £50,000 - but knowing Alfred's tastes I think that such a sum, far from being an exaggeration, might even be an understatement!"

At last the butler announces dinner. "Unreasonably late" pouts a guest. "Ah, but you see", explains another, "here the staff eats before us". "Shocking practice. Don't know what the world's coming to", says an older man, his stomach already rumbling. "But Mr de Rothschild keeps such a superb table", his friend assures him. "It's always worth the wait".

The meal, indeed, makes up for any earlier shortcomings. The sideboard is heavy with dishes made by Goodes in the Sèvres manner, banded in dark blue with gold edging, the familiar AR monogram on the rim. These form a comprehensive collection of 800 items ranging from table decorations, wineglass coolers, fruit bowls, jardinieres, coffee cups, tea cups, breakfast cups, egg cups, plates and dishes of every description. The table is tastefully lined down its centre with flowers. On the flawless white damask

Dame Nellie Melba

cloth silver scenic groups mingle with elaborate cutlery, cruet sets and an antique jewelled nef.

Jacoby's Hungarian orchestra, resplendent in Rothschild-blue coats, strikes up and its violins play softly and brilliantly in the window bay. Perhaps the grave butler is slightly concerned that one or two of his footmen are a little unsteady after their dinner, but this is soon forgotten in the serving of the meal. Prepared by the French Chef, there is soup, fish, two consecutive entrees - one perhaps of pheasants' eggs, of which Alfred had a regular supply and to which he was very partial - then joint, game - perhaps "Poussins Haltonais", - sweets and savouries, followed by fruit. The wine is the finest in the cellar and changes with the courses. During the long meal, conversation flows wittily and pleasantly, and at one point perhaps Alfred enquires of the gentlemen if they would like to hunt or shoot tomorrow, the details are decided. Then the men remain for the serious matter of the port and the ladies leave them to have coffee in a special little boudoir, where, free of former constaints, they can look out at the floodlit gardens or exchange the latest delicious scandal of the town.

The men, their port finished, then adjourn to the billiard room, or the

Moorish room next door, to smoke a cigar or a pipe, where it would not offend the delicate senses of the ladies. "Their tendency was to drawl and to affect a languid indifference to everything that was strenuous or irksome in life", Lord Hamilton comments.

This indifference disappears when the men rise early next morning to shoot or to hunt. Rabbit holes have been filled, by order of their host, lest his guests might break a leg or an ankle. Everything is arranged - horses are ready, beaters bespoken, keepers or masters prepared and a hunters' breakfast is waiting on the sideboard for their return. Pheasant shooting was overlapped by five months of fox hunting, and occasionally the hunt would go further afield for their quarry of deer or stag.

The ladies, meanwhile, sleep late and then yawn and talk in their dressing rooms or the boudoir. Few bother to read the beautifully ironed newspapers, whose dullness matches their close print. Their day begins after luncheon when the gentlemen join them. This afternoon Alfred has promised them something special. They are to see a circus - a real live circus - in the most gentle setting of Alfred's own garden.

In winter the entertainment would take place in the winter garden, but in the warmer weather, it is at the circus pavilion. Everyone has changed into afternoon dress. Alfred, resplendent in blue frock coat and lavender kid gloves, escorts his visitors to their seats beside the sanded and roped ring. It is then obvious that he is to be more than a spectator, for having seen them comfortably disposed with rugs and cushions, he then becomes ringmaster of the proceedings, complete with top hat and long whip, its handle made of lapis lazuli and gold. The little ponies trot, the horses show their paces, Lorenzo's act of animals, specially summoned from London, goes through hoops, walking on their hind legs or dancing to the background of lively music played by Alfred's own orchestra. Sometimes things do not always go according to plan.

Lady Warwick, a regular visitor, commented on one performance: "He exhibited a number of Japanese dogs, which had been taught to perform. Great confusion was aroused by the fact that, although the chief little dog performed, it was not according to the programme". However, it is all very amusing and entertaining and guests clap their appreciation in a well-bred way when Alfred comes to make his final bow.

Then to a gale of compliments, Alfred modestly conducts his guests back to the house, where tea has been prepared on the wide black and white marble terrace of the north front. Here they sit at little tables set with lace cloths and exquisite thin china, being served tea from silver teapots and tea kettles crested with the Rothschild arms; footmen and little maids in frilled caps and aprons see them well supplied with cucumber and pate sandwiches, cream scones and straw-berries, and the delightful little cakes for which Alfred's Chef is justly famed. The tinkle of tea cups vies with the splendour of the impressive fountain at the end of the garden, whose jets they watch rising and falling, while they make polite conversation.

After tea, guests withdraw to rest and make their evening toilette - fresh-frilled shirts and dresses, new jewellery and yet more flowers. This evening, as well as another superb dinner, there is to be dancing in the salon. The furniture has been removed, the carpet rolled up and the room is warm and splendid with fires and fresh flowers, the brilliant chandelier and wall fittings reflecting the light back from the tall mirrors. The orchestra, on a little stage, is almost hidden by green curtains and a green mass of plants and bushes.

Though the dancing is opened by Alfred, with one of the highest ranking ladies, in a quadrille followed by an older dance, most of the evening is soon almost exclusively devoted to the waltz. Queen Victoria herself had loved this dance though now she deplores the age as "dance mad", but then, as Doris Leslie explains, "the house party, shut off from the outside world, sang and danced, flirted and shot, hunted and fished, in a self-contained kingdom". This did not exclude more sedate activities for others who, duty done, retire to a nearby room

Winter Gardens.

for cards or to different rooms to talk scandal, romance, foreign affairs or high finance. Whatever their interests or inclinations Alfred tries to anticipate and arrange for them. Dancing however, continues until late into the night.

Next morning some of the gentlemen are up early to swim with Alfred in his plunge pool downstairs, though this is not to the taste of all. They then demolish a substantial breakfast in the dining room from a sideboard groaning with bacon, eggs, fish, meat, freshly baked continental breads, toast and conserves. A frosty morning invites them out for a sharp walk in the gardens. Here they are joined by a few early-rising ladies, attracted by the promise of skating on the ice of Alfred's large rink, which doubles in summer as an ornamental pool. Alfred

winces and rushes over in great panic if anyone falls - needing the utmost assurance that the person is really not hurt and has not sustained any injury whatsoever, before he is finally pacified.

With appetites sharpened by the morning's sport, the guests at length troop back to the house early, to enjoy one of Alfred's celebrated Sunday Luncheons. Here the house party is joined by several new guests, particularly distinguished for their wit and speeches. The meal continues well into the afternoon. Then after a due interval for rest and change of clothing, guests once more assemble in the Salon for further diversion.

Outside the house tiny carriages are lined up, drawn by little ponies handled by minute grooms in blue livery. As soon

Winter gardens north view

as the visitors have been helped in, the little grooms whip up the ponies and drive out onto the line of trees growing along the Tring-Wendover road. The scenic ride eventually ends at a pretty little Swiss Chalet in the hills. When passengers alight, they are invited to look at the kennels, where poodles, King Charles blue spaniels and pekinese are housed. Having dragged themselves away from these delights, guests are next taken to the skittles alley to play, until the housekeeper, Mrs Vince, hurries over to tell them tea is ready to be served. From the chalet balcony, or sitting room, they survey the views across the valley to the hills and the trees, while consuming a sumptuous meal. Then back to the mansion in the same little carriages to rest and change.

A further treat is in store for them when at length they sweep down, among the flowers and ferns of the main staircase, to be greeted by their host at the foot. Tonight Madame Adelina Patti has come especially from London, at Alfred's particular request, to sing for them. The chandelier is dimmed and in the shaded lights of the south drawing room, guests sink back in their comfortable padded armchairs and give themselves up to a night of art and music. This is followed by yet another superb dinner. Superlatives begin to be superfluous.

Tonight, however, after dinner, since Alfred wants to show yet another wonder to his celebrated artiste, he offers to take everybody up to see the Belvedere. Some of the ladies nervously decline, but Madame Patti, with other guests, braves

the four storeys to reach the little viewing pavilion at the top of the house. Here, open to the air and under the stars, they can see the floodlit house and grounds, and in the distance catch the twinkling lights of Aylesbury and the villages. Alfred also proudly picks out the lights marking the houses of his other Rothschild relatives nearby.

Then down to a warming punch and more music. This time Alfred takes up an ivory baton set with a ring of diamonds to conduct his orchestra himself - mainly Viennese waltzes, Gilbert and Sullivan melodies and popular tunes - proving that he is, in the eyes of his guests, truly a man of many talents. This starts off some impromptu dancing, much enjoyed by all. Before the guests, tired but contented, retire to bed, one remarks out of their host's hearing, that he hopes the heavy tread of the security policeman, guarding Alfred's treasures, will not disturb their slumbers again tonight.

Next morning, after a late breakfast, the carriages come rolling up the drive to take away the guests. They are loaded down with huge boxes of fruit, flowers, chocolates, cakes, perhaps a souvenir book of the house and presents. Alfred takes his farewell of his guests, making them feel that it was he that had been honoured by their visit and that devoting himself to their every wish and pleasure had been his greatest privilege. On their side, his guests all agree that they had never before enjoyed such a diverting and enjoyable visit and maybe hope that this will not be the last time they will be entertained at Halton House.

CHAPTER 2

ALFRED'S FAMILY

"Peace has her victories, No less renown'd than war" Milton

Alfred Charles was a member of the powerful and wealthy Banking Family of Rothschild, the great grandson of its founder and the grandson of the first 'English' Rothschild. It was because of his inherited wealth and position that he was able to contemplate the creation of such a house as Halton.

MAYER AMSCHEL 1744 -1812

The family fortunes began in the middle of the eighteenth century with Mayer Amschel, who was born in 1744 in the Jewish Ghetto of Frankfurt-on-the-Main, a city at the heart of European commerce. Several generations before, an ancestor had nailed a red badge over his doorway, thus becoming known as 'das Rote Schildt', which evolved into the family surname of Rothschild. Orphaned at eleven, Mayer eventually left for Hanover and a cousin placed him in an Oppenheimer Bank as a clerk. Here the boy's keen brain and endless capacity for hard work, together with a growing interest in antique coins and their trade value, fired his ambitions and drew such attention to his talents that, when he was barely twenty, he was encouraged to return to Frankfurt to become a dealer in rare coins and various other kinds of

...WHEN HE WAS BARELY TWENTY, HE WAS ENCOURAGED TO RETURN TO FRANKFURT TO BECOME A DEALER IN RARE COINS AND VARIOUS OTHER KINDS OF MERCHANDISE.

merchandise. One of his more distinguished patrons was the wealthy Prince William of Hesse, who eventually awarded Mayer the appointment of Crown Agent.

On the strength of this, he married. When both family and trade grew, he moved to accommodation more suitable for his expanding business. In later years Prince William became Landgrave and Mayer was increasingly involved in state transactions. Thus he set out on the road which his descendants were to follow with such success, for he had five sons. These five sons are represented by the five arrows of the Rothschild badge. They became his agents in Europe, settling eventually, one at home in Germany, and the other four in the capital cities of Austria, Naples in Italy, France and England, where they founded their own family dynasties.

The Napoleonic Wars threw unexpected opportunities in Mayer's way. He managed to salvage part of Prince William's possessions and used them to his own advantage during the Prince's enforced exile by Napoleon, but ultimately he was able to return the capital to a grateful Prince. Speedy exchange of money and information through his gradually spreading family, a talent for taking the right chance, hard work and a reputation for scrupulous honesty put Mayer in the first rank of international bankers and millionaires.

His sons developed what he had begun.

NATHAN MAYER 1777 -1836

Mayer's third son was the family's plump, red-haired financial genius. He came to England in 1798 and started business in Manchester, dealing principally in cotton goods.

Soon he had moved to London, where he registered at New Court in St. Swithin's Lane, as a Merchant Banker. From this address the Rothschild Bank still operates today.

Nathan had a firm belief in the ultimate victory of England in its struggle against Napoleon. His private and efficient communication service

Cartoon of Nathan Mayer Rothschild

maintained England's lifeline in Europe. Rothschild funds were sent to assist England's Allies, unsuspected by the French, and Nathan earned the gratitude of the Government of the day. In 1806 he became a naturalised British citizen.

Thus the dynasty was established and the London Banking House maintained and extended its influence in England and on the Continent. The strength of the family, as always, was to be its sons and there was much inter-marriage to keep their money and influence within the family.

Shortly before his death Nathan bought Gunnersbury Park during the period of the agricultural depression of the 1830s. This became the first Rothschild country house and was much frequented by his children. Later, his widow bought a little land at Mentmore in Buckinghamshire.

THE ROTHSCHILD FAMILY TREE
(English Branch)

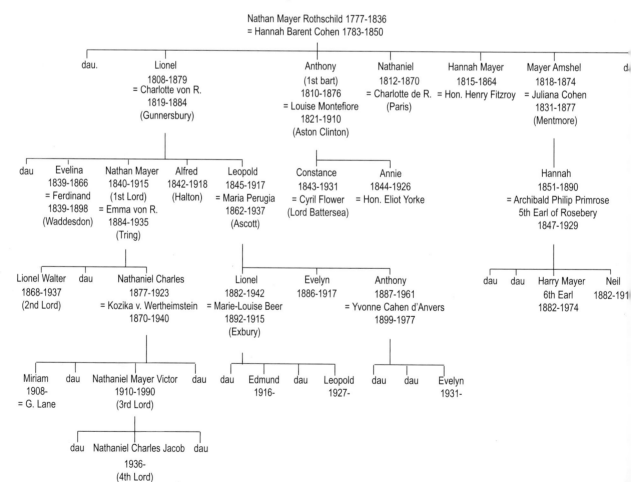

Nathan Mayer Rothschild 1777-1836
= Hannah Barent Cohen 1783-1850

dau.

Lionel
1808-1879
= Charlotte von R.
1819-1884
(Gunnersbury)

Anthony
(1st bart)
1810-1876
= Louise Montefiore
1821-1910
(Aston Clinton)

Nathaniel
1812-1870
= Charlotte de R.
(Paris)

Hannah Mayer
1815-1864
= Hon. Henry Fitzroy

Mayer Amshel
1818-1874
= Juliana Cohen
1831-1877
(Mentmore)

dau.

dau

Evelina
1839-1866
= Ferdinand
1839-1898
(Waddesdon)

Nathan Mayer
1840-1915
(1st Lord)
= Emma von R.
1884-1935
(Tring)

Alfred
1842-1918
(Halton)

Leopold
1845-1917
= Maria Perugia
1862-1937
(Ascott)

Constance
1843-1931
= Cyril Flower
(Lord Battersea)

Annie
1844-1926
= Hon. Eliot Yorke

Hannah
1851-1890
= Archibald Philip Primrose
5th Earl of Rosebery
1847-1929

Lionel Walter
1868-1937
(2nd Lord)

dau

Nathaniel Charles
1877-1923
= Kozika v. Wertheimstein
1870-1940

Lionel
1882-1942
= Marie-Louise Beer
1892-1915
(Exbury)

Evelyn
1886-1917

Anthony
1887-1961
= Yvonne Cahen d'Anvers
1899-1977

dau

dau

Harry Mayer
6th Earl
1882-1974

Neil
1882-191

Miriam
1908-
= G. Lane

dau

Nathaniel Mayer Victor
1910-1990
(3rd Lord)

dau

dau

Edmund
1916-

dau

Leopold
1927-

dau

dau

Evelyn
1931-

dau

Nathaniel Charles Jacob
1936-
(4th Lord)

dau

LIONEL 1808-1879

Nathan had four sons. Lionel, the first-born, followed the path marked out by his immigrant father, as head of the English Bank, but each of his brothers became a partner, following the motto of the baronetcy that their Austrian Uncle had acquired in 1822. It ran "Concordia, integritas, industria" - "harmony, honesty and diligence".

During Lionel's lifetime loans were made to the British Government culminating in an almost overnight loan of four million pounds to enable Prime Minister Disraeli to buy shares of the Suez Canal sold by the Khedive of Egypt. It is interesting to note that in 1914 these shares were valued at £40 million, and that this investment in the years before the 1939 War brought the Exchequer over two million pounds a year. Most of the home and foreign transactions of the Rothschild Bank during this period met with equal success, so that the family fortunes continued to flourish.

Lionel inherited Gunnersbury Park but preferred his London house. Nevertheless, persuaded to take up hunting in the Vale of Aylesbury for his health, he eventually acquired Tring Park and the land at Halton.

ALFRED CHARLES 1842 -1918

Lionel's three sons, Nathaniel, Alfred Charles and Leopold followed in their father's footsteps not only in banking but in having property both in London and the country. Nathaniel, the eldest son and future Lord Rothschild, inherited Tring. Leopold was given Ascott. Halton passed to Alfred Charles, the middle son, and to him we owe Halton House.

Early Life

Alfred was born in 1842. After an early education at home, where his gifts in music, drama and languages were noted and encouraged, he continued his schooling at King's College, London. At this time legislation barred students from Universities, unless they belonged to the Church of England. Cambridge, how-ever, unlike most Universities, did not enforce this exclusion until an under-graduate was about to be awarded his degree. Alfred was therefore sent with his younger brother Leopold to Trinity College, Cambridge, to study for a degree in mathematics. It so happened that the Prince of Wales, Albert Edward, the son and heir of Queen Victoria, was a fellow student at the same time. Thus a friendship was formed which lasted throughout their lives and was to be of mutual pleasure and benefit.

At twenty-one Alfred joined the staff at New Court to learn the business of Banking from his father. He also did the equivalent of the Grand Tour - visiting Europe, where he could stay with his innumerable relations, finding out at first-hand about countries, people, politics and business, as well as building up a fund of useful contacts for the future.

Vanity Fair cartoon of Leopold de Rothschild.

Appearance

By now Alfred was a young man of considerable ability and talents. He spoke French and German like a native, played the piano and other instruments, and cultivated all the social graces. Unlike his brothers, he was slim, blue-eyed and fair with elegant, sandy sidewhiskers, first trimmed into the fashionable 'dundreary' style and later into the neat 'favouris' favoured by the Edwardians. He was the 'smallest and most refined' of the brothers. Mrs Lionel de Rothschild, the wife of his nephew, describes him as a 'dapper little man very elegant, as though he came out of the frames of one of his eighteenth-century portraits'. He dressed and carried himself well, being somewhat dashing in his youth, his taste quietening down with the more sober colours and styles of the Edwardians. Nevertheless, at all times, he paid particular attention to the flowers in his button-hole. His brothers were sometimes rather shaken by their flamboyance, which did not always accord with their surroundings. Leopold once had to run after Alfred to make him change a particularly colourful creation, before attending a synagogue. (Alfred remained moderately faithful to his Jewish beliefs and customs, although

Vanity Fair cartoon of Alfred de Rothschild.

Waddesdon, The Rothschild

Collection (The National Trust).

Photo: Mike Fear

never aspiring to leadership of the Jewish community). He retained a great fondness for clothes, being something of a dandy, with a definite preference for his cat's eye tie-pin and a range of walking sticks topped with gold or tortoiseshell and various stones.

As a young man, when he first appeared at Aston Clinton in a suit of brown velveteen, his aunt remarked "What a charming picture of youth and good spirits".

Even when sick, grey and old he dressed impeccably, no doubt owing to the careful administrations of his valet, who travelled with him whether he stayed at Seamore Place or visited Folkestone, Halton, a Spa in Austria or a relation in Paris.

Personality

Alfred was born to a position of great wealth and a tradition of hard work. The Rothschild genes were his birthright, together with an embarrassment of other talents - often found with high intelligence - so that his life was a perpetual struggle between the stern dictates of duty and sybaritic pleasure in beauty and the arts. This led to his being regarded by the Rothschilds as something of a black sheep.

In his earlier years pleasures were an escape route, though later he generally found a way of reconciling duties and pleasures. This may explain the puzzling extremes or contradictions to be met in such things as his choice of pictures and in the many habits dubbed eccentricities by his contemporaries.

On first encounter, outsiders were confronted by a slight, elegant man of shy charm, diffidence and undeniable knowledge and ability, who wanted to be liked by everyone. This was the more attractive, as a complete contrast to the exhausting ebullience of one brother and the austere almost harsh dedication of the other. "Mr Alfred had money in plenty to spare, but he knew how to spend it in helping to give others happiness" said Mrs Clement Scott. As Alfred matured, he learned to spice his pleasure with humour, his introversion and shyness with affability and an affectionate nature and growing store of knowledge with a becoming modesty. Truly at ease only in the presence of those he knew well he remained loyal to, and retained, a widening circle of friends and staff. This fuelled his social ambition to show his family that he could succeed, by collecting notabilities and celebrities as others collected butterflies. At heart, he had a strong sense of family loyalty and was always sensitive to its opinion and influence, but this did not prevent him acting independently.

Nevertheless, though perpetually occupied by bank or social affairs, Alfred emerges as an essentially lonely man. The search for activity and distraction had an almost frantic intensity. This symptom frequently manifests itself in the powerful or the wealthy, who fear that any friendship is for the wrong reasons and is not for themselves alone. As a result they suffer isolation, often caused by what they most fear, and are accused of aloofness, often misinterpreted as pride. This explains Alfred's almost pathetic eagerness to help or to please, and the extreme lengths to which he would go to do so, yet he discounted all thanks to the extent that, even when making his most generous gestures, he preferred to remain anonymous and, if possible, absent when they took place. This charming, gentle, witty exterior sometimes gave the impression that Alfred was no more than a dilettante but there is evidence to the contrary.

Work

Throughout his lifetime Alfred worked at the Bank, although he frequently kept his staff after hours because, unlike his brothers, he rarely arrived until late in the morning. Nevertheless, Alfred took part in all the normal work and was as much consulted and advised as his brothers. Decisions in all important international financial transactions were only made by the three partners in conjunction, which can be seen by the voluminous daily correspondence of all three brothers. It is noticeable, however, that each has his own style. Alfred's letters, for instance, tend to include snippets of family, racing or political news, along with more weighty matters. His tone is less brusque and more diplomatic. Although he was no reader - as evidenced by the diminutive size of his library at Halton, it was said of him that he knew how to pick the brains of those with whom he came into contact, and many were the best brains in the country.

In later life it was noticed that Alfred had two groups of friends. One was the social set from Marlborough House, including the Prince of Wales, and the most celebrated artistes and beauties of the era; the other was taken from the world of politics and power. It ranged from Lord Kitchener, Disraeli (an old friend of the family), Prime Minister Asquith whom Alfred visited every morning at one period, to foreign diplomats such as the Marquis de Soveral the Portuguese ambassador, and Baron Von Echardstein, Secretary to the German Embassy, both very close friends.

At twenty-six he became the youngest director of the Bank of England, a post which he held from 1869 to 1889. This was an honour but no sinecure. The Illustrated American Journal comments that "He is remembered as the only Director who, when he visited the Western Branch at Burlington Gardens to examine bonds and securities, made a practice of bringing a box of cigars with him for the delectation of the clerks". He retained the Directorship for over twenty years and only resigned when, by virtue of this office, he discovered and made public the exorbitant profit being made by a dealer in selling him a picture.

In the city he was recognised as a particularly reliable and alert financier. In 1892 he was selected to join a delegation of five sent by the British Government to the International Monetary Conference in Brussels, to which the USA sent observers, while India, Greece, Denmark, Austria, Hungary and other major European countries took part. Characteristically, Alfred arrived with mounds of luggage and 4 valets. The Americans could not believe their eyes, though they conceded that he united amiability with ability! Alfred put forward the proposals for

Great Britain as well as a suggestion of his own. Though not all the proposals were accepted, Alfred was one of the signatories of the Conference Report in 1893. Of particular note was his advice to the British Government after the outbreak of World War I, which assisted in disentangling German and British financial affairs, but he was involved in many other delicate transactions which have remained secret.

Diplomacy

He was always well informed, particularly in foreign affairs - not surprising considering there were members of the Rothschild family scattered all over Europe, many involved in intimate business deals with the English Bank. His fluency in foreign languages no doubt arose from, and considerably assisted in, this interest but also gradually drew him in as negotiator between Britain and other nations on an informal level. Such activities ranged from meetings between Count Hatzfeld (the German Ambassador) and Mr Chamberlain (the Colonial Secretary) at Alfred's house, to an admittance by Alfred himself that "I have always been more or less behind the scenes" ... and "I have done everything possible over a long period of years".

Indeed the years 1890 to 1914 were riddled with crises big and small, involving the interests and acquisitions, both territorial and commercial, of the Great Powers of Germany, Austria, France, Russia and China. Great Britain with her widespread colonies was at the centre of it all. Minor wars or incidents flared up regularly. The main aim of all diplomats was to prevent quarrels involving two Great Powers from drawing in others and destroying the balance of power in Europe. Such delicate negotiations called for special skills and careful diplomacy. There was the South African (Boer) War, the Port Arthur incident, the Bundesrath incident, and crises over Samoa, Egypt and China. In all these, by secret meetings, letters, influence and plain blunt speaking, Alfred was very much involved, using his tenacious memory

Disraeli

and his special knowledge and skills to interfere with, and if possible prevent, the growth of many serious situations. There is no doubt that unobtrusively Alfred de Rothschild played a considerable part in keeping the peace of Europe.

A paper on Anglo-German relationships in the first decade of the 20th Century pays tribute to his achievements.

"In fact, it was Mr Alfred de Rothschild who became the principal and most powerful champion for the understanding between England and Germany. He always used his influence in favour of it and on a great many occasions when the relations between the two countries became somewhat strained, he helped to smooth matters over and rendered great services not only to his own country but also to Germany".

A flavour of his diplomacy and style shows in this extract from a letter written in 1898:

"In a word, of recent years, Germany's policy towards England has been a kind of 'pinprick' policy, and, although a pin is not a very impressive instrument, repeated pricks may cause a wound... Possibly you can prevail upon his Excellency to send me a few lines in reply to my observations; I would naturally show these only in the highest circles, and make the most discreet use of them."

In addition, although he had inherited the position of Imperial and Royal AustroHungarian Consul-General, he took pride in the title and aimed to justify it. For a century his family had trusted and been trusted in Austria, however, the First World War was to destroy Alfred's trust, while his pride in the Austrian connection was to be shattered. At the other end of the scale, he greatly valued his French Knighthood of the Legion d'Honour and The Companion of the Victorian Order which King Edward VII awarded him as a sign of appreciation for his efforts on Great Britain's behalf.

Communications

Because of his English appearance, in addition to his work at the bank, he increasingly found himself representing his family in public, whether receiving Princes, interviewing ambassadors or taking part in social engagements. He had a way with words and could speak in public with aplomb. Even at fifteen, the speech he made at his sister's wedding was remarked upon as unusually adroit for such a young man. He could be witty and funny in anecdote or repartee and this facility never left him, whether it was conducting an amusing conversation in company or contributing a clever trifle to the magazine 'Punch'.

Art

In artistic matters Alfred considered himself a connoisseur, but whereas his taste in architecture and furnishings may be questioned, he certainly did display a very personal taste and talent in his fine art collection. He explained his criteria to Edgar Everington.

"In the first place I do not think that the value and attraction of a picture consists solely in the fact of its having been painted or attributed to some very great master. It ought to have some intrinsic merits per se, either as regards beauty of the subject or, if a portrait, the beauty or characteristic features of the person represented, or if a landscape, the depth and breadth of expression, that is to say the true representation of nature; but if the picture does not appeal to the eye and does not draw the attention of either the amateur or the expert, then it fails to be a thing of beauty which is a joy for ever and sinks into the insignificance it deserves". He appreciated landscapes and portraits and could quite happily swing from severely simple to the emotionally florid. His likes encompassed subjects as far apart as ragged peasants, voluptuous nudes and aristocratic courtiers. In fact, his taste ran to rather unexpected extremes.

His collection, however, was not merely a rich man's whim. At the beginning it was selected carefully, within the fairly narrow limits of the seventeenth century French and English painters favoured by his family. These he started gathering in his youth, when he bought for his father's collection, paintings which, it was understood, would later pass to him. This was how he acquired 'Le Baisser Envoye' in the Boudoir at Halton and the portrait of 'Lady Hamilton' by Romney which he kept in his Red Room, as well as many smaller Dutch works. However, he added steadily to his collection throughout his life, selling as well as buying, particularly when large bodies of fine works appeared, as in the Sale of the Estates of Lord Lonsdale in 1885 and Lord Ashburton in 1907 - a task in which he was greatly assisted by his art advisors and close friends, Sir Guy Laking, Charles Davis and Sir Joshua Duveen.

Portrait of Lady Hamilton by Romney kept in the Red Room

Later his tastes broadened and he broke away from the Schools traditionally popular with the Rothschilds, and started to include Italian artists which, because of their religious content, his family avoided. Thus he acquired some superb works attributed to Bellini, Boticelli, Titian, Veronese, Bronzino, Domenichino, Leonardo and Raphael, amongst others. In the same way pictures by a few Spanish painters such as Velasquez and Murillo and the German Durer, found their way into his hands.

His houses, in London at Seamore Place and here at Halton, were full of paintings. Halton House was built partly to provide suitable settings for his collection. At Halton he displayed Gainsborough and Reynolds, portraits, and one of the drawing rooms was named the Lawrence Room because it contained an exceptionally fine work by this painter. The dining room was called the Bamfylde Room, after the lady, painted by Reynolds, whose portrait dominated it. He had an unfortunate affection for Greuze and Boucher, whose 'pretty work' proliferated in the salon and boudoir - Alfred having gathered more pieces by Boucher than anyone else in the United Kingdom, except the Wallace Collection. When his taste expanded, he dubbed another room the Bronzino Room, where he kept Italian paintings and other works.

A feature of Alfred's collection, showing how far ahead he was of his contemporaries in many things, was not only in his care for his pictures but in the introduction of special electric lighting for each picture. Such innovation was a revelation. Mrs Erskine, a visitor in 1902, was most impressed.

"We find pictures that are above suspicion, well hung, in excellent preservation and so well lighted that, by means of a powerful electric light placed over each frame, they can be studied in the darkest .... of weather".

The house also contained part of his collection of fine French furniture, clocks, vases, china, candelabra, statues and little objects ranging from cups to carvings - many dating from the reigns of the Kings Louis XIV to XVI. "The Rothschilds owned more of their furniture than the three Kings together", quipped one commentator.

Another story current was that Alfred and Ferdinand, his cousin, had both agreed to try to bring back the taste and decoration of the French eighteenth century. They thus consciously used Halton and Waddesdon as show-cases in pursuing this objective. The partial success, of at least Alfred's plan, can be gauged from Dorothy Neville's assessment of him as:

"the finest amateur judge in England of Eighteenth-Century French art". There were tables by Reisener and Gouthière, commodes by Dubois, other French furniture in marquetry and ebony, and garnitures of Sèvres, Meissen and Limoges porcelain. These surrounded Alfred in rich profusion, together with Gobelins and Beauvais tapestries, silk

Portrait of Lady Paulett by Romney, later paired with Lady Hamilton in the Red Room

and damask hangings and Turkish or Persian rugs. Morton dryly ascribes the 'Rothschild Style' in the public mind to:

"Bourbon meubles sprinkled with Renaissance bibelots and an opulence of ormolu and boiseries" a description which fits Alfred's Halton home very neatly.

Decorating his houses appropriately, however, was not Alfred's only involvement in the world of art. He became one of the Trustees of the National Gallery, to which he willed one of his finest paintings by Reynolds, and was a founder trustee of the Wallace Collection, to which he gave a magnificent series of lustres and chandeliers. He also supplemented government grants, when they were not large enough, to buy important pictures which he felt should be in the National Collection, such as works by Velasquez, Franz Hals, Holbein and Moroni. He also acquired the fourteenth century 'Pichon Cup' for the British Museum.

Music

Alfred was extremely fond of music. In his early years he played the piano - a hobby which was to give him and others pleasure in the years to come. It was noted on one occasion that Alfred remained playing his piano until late at night alone with the Prince of Wales, to beguile the troubled Prince, who that day had appeared in court in a case connected with one of the scandals that rocked Marlborough House. Alfred also favoured the violin and even ventured into playing the 'Orchestrion' - an instrument much deplored by his friends and staff. At Halton he maintained an orchestra which he occasionally conducted rather amateurishly.

He rented a nightly box at Covent Garden during the Opera season, which he generously shared with friends. He often invited the greatest stars to entertain or be entertained at 'professional dinners' and these were showered afterwards with valuable gifts. Singers such as Melba, Patti, Niccolini, the two De Reszkes and Alvarez performed for him, together with famous violinists such as Mischa Elman, Sarasate, and Ysaye or pianists and composers such as Rubinstein and Liszt, most of whom figure in his invitation book at Halton. It was Alfred who arranged the Gala Night at Covent Garden in aid of charities for the Boer War and had the temerity to direct that prices up to £250 should be charged for seats and boxes.

Theatre

Music and the theatre were his twin delights. Indeed, if he showed any preferences, then by his love of the dramatic and by his eccentricities - rather highly coloured for an otherwise modest, rather introvert personality - he displayed that it was with the world of drama and showmanship he was most at home. No doubt today he could have been an impressario.

From acting at school and University, he became a devotee and benefactor of the theatre. Apart from being a regular theatre-goer, he at one time became a partner in both the Gaiety Theatre and the Empire - enabling him to invite individual current stars to his occasional Adoration Dinners. At another time he supported Lily Langtry's request for money on a production at the Prince's Theatre. He rarely missed a dress rehearsal or first night at these or other theatres, usually occupying the same box and wearing the most brilliant scarlet buttonhole of carnations.

He was also charitably open-handed to the Actors' Orphanage and in setting up trust funds to help famous theatre personalities when they became old or sick.

Animals

His fondness for animals found expression in many ways. He bred King Charles blue and white spaniels, whose kennels his guests often visited at the Swiss Chalet on the hillside near Halton House. He himself often carried a pet dog, usually a poodle and sometimes two, wherever he went and in London he kept a pet goat, which caused traffic chaos when it escaped. Pheasants were bred on his estate at Halton, while Chinese deer and peacocks wandered freely in his grounds. Though he was never a keen sportsman - it was noticed that he avoided joining a hunt whenever possible - he occupied his obligatory place at race meetings and was considered a popular, even enthusiastic, supporter of guns. He prized a pair of Purdey guns and owned many other of quality and fine workmanship. He took a genuine interest in horses and ponies - he kept many in his circus and stables. It was he who introduced a new foreign breed, the beautiful golden Palomino pony into this country.

Transport

It was some time before Alfred became interested in cars. Being of a nervous disposition, his tastes veered to the conservative and safe means of transport. But when he eventually succumbed to the fashion, he had not one but five cars in his Halton garages - a Wolseley, two Renaults, a Zedal Phaeton and an Elswick, all in the famous Rothschild yellow and blue colours, each with its own chauffeur. Nevertheless, he did not leave anything to chance and in the early years he frequently had his car followed by a carriage, later by another car, as insurance against breakdowns. In addition, he rented his own railway carriage for the use of himself and his guests.

Health

Alfred's nervous disposition became more marked as he grew older, so that he became almost a hypochondriac. In his middle-age he developed a digestive disorder, which despite employing the best chef in London, could result in his presiding over a magnificent meal where he was hardly able to eat anything. He was abstemious with wine for the same reason, but what he drank was of the best. He enjoyed the advice of several of the most eminent doctors when he resided in London, while paying a retaining fee for consultation outside the city.

He also had a weak heart, and therefore had to be careful to avoid occasions involving too much activity or stress. This resulted in some amusing incidents, such as when his doctors insisted on the exercise of walking to work, Alfred arranged to be followed by a vehicle, in case he became too tired or felt faint, a frequent occurrence. Another foible was the bottle of smelling salts he always kept close at hand.

Once, after an 'Adoration Dinner' given by Alfred in honour of Lily Langtry, her host asked Lily what gift she would like, intending to give her a valuable pre-selected one. She, however, picked up the prize of Alfred's snuff boxes. "He had a weak heart", she confessed "and for a moment I thought I had stopped it." However, all was well. Alfred recovered, retrieved his collector's piece and Lily received one of the usual gift boxes instead.

There is no doubt that Alfred appreciated the extra attention and sympathy he gained from his ailments, but their result was that he always travelled with a collection of remedies near to hand and never put on weight. It is said that the bottles in his medicine cabinet rivalled in quantity and price those in his wine cellar.

Heirs

Few could accuse him of dereliction of duty, however eccentric his artistic whims, except in the matter of marriage, although his liking for women was well-known. Either he mistrusted his capacity to inspire genuine affection until it was too late, or simply there was no suitable Jewish bride available. He was the only one of the three brothers to remain unmarried and his Rothschild heir was his nephew Lionel.

Nevertheless, he appears to have left several so-called God-children and sought to provide for them, in contra-diction of the customary dictates of the family. His favourite, never acknowledged openly, but as an adult often accompanying him abroad and acting as his hostess, was Almina Wombwell. She became Lady Carnarvon and later inherited Alfred's London property, furnishings and paintings. In this way some of Alfred's fortune came to be used in financing the Egyptian Venture of Lord Carnarvon, who was backing Howard Carter's excavations in the Valley of the Kings. This was to result in the discovery of Tutankhamen's tomb and its incredible treasures. After her husband's death, Lady Carnarvon remained interested in the excavation.

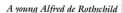

A young Alfred de Rothschild

Waddesdon, The Rothschild Collection

(Rothschild Family Trust).

Photo: Mike Fear

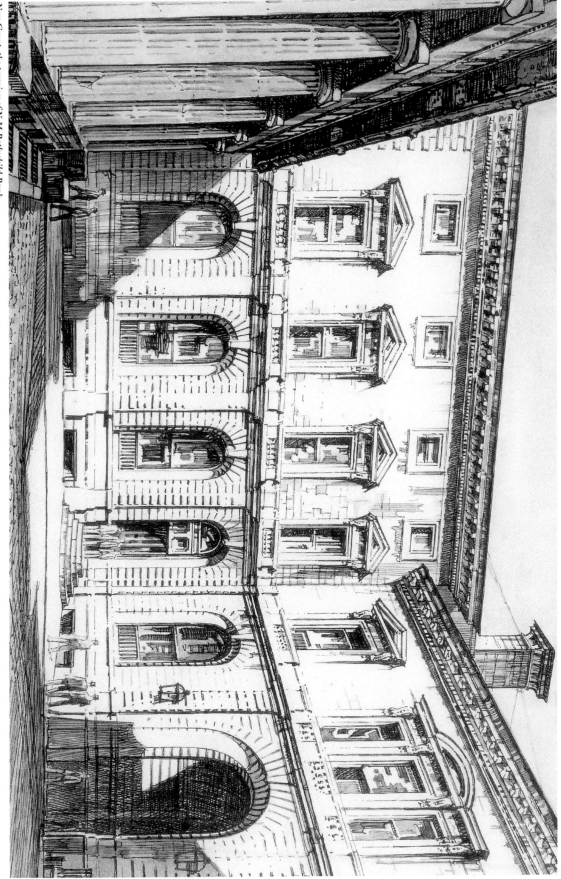

New Court, the premises of N.M Rothschild Bank

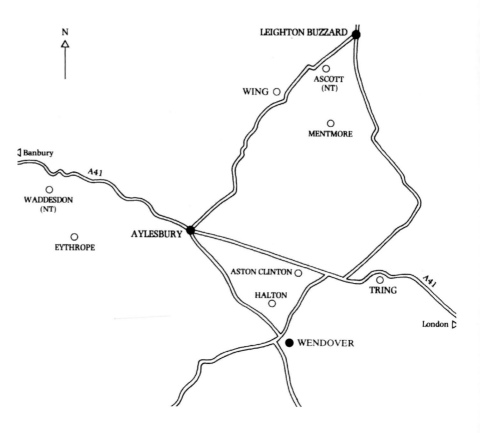

THE ROTHSCHILDS

IN THE VALE OF AYLESBURY

The much inter-married Rothschild family built five prodigy houses around Aylesbury during the mid 19th century of which only one survives in its original state. (Times)

The nineteenth-century Rothschilds owned much property, including opulent town houses in London - most within a stone's throw of each other. The men, however, ran to weight, so it was as much to counter this tendency as to take them out of the Bank at weekends, that the four sons of Nathan de Rothschild - the founder of the English family - took up the socially acceptable sport of hunting in the Vale of Aylesbury using a pack of foxhounds from Hastoe in the woods above Tring. In time they switched to stag-hunting, bringing along their own quarry, since the native fox, naturally averse to the entertainment of being caught and killed, was frequently uncooperative enough to escape.

The sporting interest of the four brothers in Buckinghamshire was re-inforced by other considerations.

Knowing the immense difficulties facing a foreign Jewish family in breaking into accepted and ruling social circles, they were advised to concentrate together on the same area of country, where by sheer numbers and benefactions they could no longer be ignored.

The economy of the day played into their hands. In 1846 the repeal of the Corn Laws lowered the cost of land and its legal ownership was extended to members of other faiths outside the Church of England. In any case, Lionel and his brothers could not resist bargains, particularly when they offered a solution to their sporting and social aspirations. Further depressed farm prices in the 1870s following the introduction of fast steamships and refrigeration, again tempted the family to invest in still more land.

THUS BY ACCIDENT AND DESIGN THE ROTHSCHILDS CAME TO OWN SOME OF THE LARGEST ESTATES IN THE AYLESBURY VALE.

Thus by accident and design the Rothschilds came to own some of the largest estates in the Aylesbury Vale. This did not, of course, prevent acquisitions elsewhere but Buckinghamshire's proximity to London made it an ideal area from all points of view

The results were spectacular. As the years passed, the Rothschilds acquired membership of the House of Commons, the bench, the county, a title and - the final accolade - the friendship of the Prince of Wales. The doors of society opened wide. They were accepted.

Many of the estates purchased by the Rothschilds were furnished with large houses, some of which are still open to the public.

Mentmore

Mentmore Estate came chiefly from Captain Harcourt's daughter Julia in 1836 and was purchased by Mayer. Mentmore

Aston Clinton Estate

Towers was designed by Paxton and Stokes in the style of the Elizabethan Wollaton Hall. It was begun in 1850 and passed to Mayer's only daughter Hannah, who later married Lord Rosebery. Following a sale which generated great local interest, it was bought by the Religious Order of World Government for the Age of Enlightenment. More recent plans include conversion to a five-star hotel.

Aston Clinton

Aston Clinton Estate was bought from Viscount Lake by Anthony in 1851. The house was designed by Devey in an Italianate style and begun in 1874. It passed to Anthony's daughter Constance, who married Cyril Flower, Lord Battersea. It later became a boys' school, a country club, a hotel and offices before being demolished in the 1950s.

Tring

Tring Estate was bought by Lionel in 1872 from Sir Drummond Smith. Tring Park was originally designed by Christopher Wren for Henry Guy, a Gentleman of the Privy Chamber to Charles II. Today it looks like an eighteenth century European mansion, after Devey greatly altered and extended it over a long period of time, and the building is currently an Arts Council School.

Ascott

Mayer bought Ascott Estate from Lord Overstone in 1873, but it was soon passed to Lionel's son, Leopold who added to it. Ascott House began life as two-bedroomed cottage in 1873, was extended and added to, mainly in Jacobean half-timbered, long, low style, by first Devey and then Williams. It is now held by the National Trust and is open to the public.

Waddesdon

Waddesdon and Winchendon Estates

Tring Estate

were bought in 1874 from the Duke of Marlborough by Ferdinand of the Austrian branch of the family. Begun in 1875, Waddesdon Manor was designed by Destailleur in the style of a French Chateau. The grounds were extensively landscaped, resulting in spectacular gardens, views and woodlands. The village of Waddesdon contains many exceptional examples of "Rothschild architecture" and the Manor itself has been given to the National Trust.

Eyethrope

Home to Alice Rothschild, sister to Ferdinand, Eyethrope Pavilion was designed by Devey and begun in 1876.

It is smaller, a mixture of French Renaissance and Tudor styles and remains in private hands.

Halton

When Alfred took over the Halton Estate in 1880 there was no suitable house for him to use as a residence.

The former Halton House had been positioned in the village of Halton, a little west of the Church. Old maps show it with orchards, a large park, gardens, lawns and fountains. In later years the grounds were bisected by the Grand Junction Canal. Over earlier centuries, house and estate had passed through the hands of various families, who sometimes occupied and occasionally leased them. The house itself was thus subjected to much rebuilding and alteration as architectural fashions changed.

Before Henry VIII, the land of the manor had belonged to the Monastery of Christchurch, Canterbury, but following the Dissolution of the Monasteries, it was bought in 1545 by the Bradshawes. As this was the golden age of Tudor building, it is fair to assume that a house had by then been built, if one did not exist before.

From then it passed briefly to the Winchcombes and, eventually through

Mentmore Estate

marriage to the heiress of the rich merchant family of Fermors. They were absentee landlords, so that by 1706 the house, now exhibiting a fashionable, Palladian style, curved frontage, was leased to the Dashwood family.

In 1720, James Fermor finally sold house and estate to Francis Dashwood, known later as the Sir Francis connected with the Hellfire Club of West Wycombe. At this time, the building was described as elegant and inviting but gradually it deteriorated, until in the time of the grandson of Sir Francis, it only rates the description of 'plain and unostentatious', although even at this point, there seems to be a general consensus on the fine views it enjoyed across the Vale of Aylesbury.

Sir John Dashwood King was the last of the family in residence, and after his

death, the house, now known locally as the Dashwood Mansion, was unoccupied.

In June 1849, Sir John's eldest son, Sir George Dashwood, auctioned off the contents. The Catalogue of sale covers all the household furniture, linen, oil paintings and prints, 1,200 ounces of silver plate, 1,500 books, brewing plant and farm stock. Deserted and stripped of all furnishings, the house rapidly fell into decay.

It was sold with the major part of the estate in 1853 to Baron Lionel de Rothschild.

During the following years Lionel gradually acquired any privately owned properties standing within the boundaries of the manor. One of these was the local inn beside Halton churchyard, whose innkeeper stubbornly refused to

Waddesdon Manor

sell, until, overtaken by illness, he was pensioned off to spend his remaining days in part of the now deserted Dashwood Mansion. It appears that this is the last time that anyone lived in in the old house. The inn itself was absorbed into Lionel's property in 1862, although, ironically, it was destroyed by fire in 1866.

By this time Halton House had deteriorated still further, and was finally demolished after Alfred had taken over his father's estate. Records of the sale of the remnants appear in his early 1880 accounts.

So ended the first Halton House.

CHAPTER 4

South Aspect 1883

ALFRED BUILDS

Halton Mansion . . . adds another to the many palatial homes of the Rothschilds in Bucks and must now be numbered as one of the most imposing of them. Bucks Herald

With the old house gone, a new Halton House was therefore a necessity. The idea must have been in hand by 1880. A fine site had been chosen among some of the most glorious beechwoods in England. It was still at Halton but this time on a commanding eminence and slope of the hill above the village, sheltered by the Chilterns, and away from the first house, the name of which, however, it preserved.

The work was entrusted to William Cubbitt and Company under the direct control of their head man, William R. Rogers. Indeed, Mr Rogers or Rodriguez, may also have been the architect, since he was the design partner in the firm and appears to have designed a house for Leopold Rothschild at Hamilton Place in the early 1880's.

A craftsman's name survives high on a lead moulding of the roof - Ben Battson - probably a lead worker, who carved his name in this inaccessible spot, together with the date May 20, 1884.

Alfred sometimes presented, as a souvenir to special visitors, a blue leather, monogrammed album containing photographs of the house. One such is still in the keeping of the Mess and is inscribed: "To William R Rogers Esq. with every expression of sincere gratitude. From Alfred de Rothschild 11 May 1888."

Despite its size the house appears to have taken only about 3 years to build and employed a veritable army of workmen. It was finished in July 1883 but had to await its grand opening until the following year.

An early photograph of the rear of the house records work in progress. In the background, part of the house is still in scaffolding, with the staff ceremonially lined up on the terrace. To the fore are gardeners in shirtsleeves and bowler hats, an interesting sidelight on manners of the late 19th century.

Alfred believed in instant gardening, being too impatient to await nature's results. Trees were therefore planted full grown and many plants and shrubs, appeared in one place one day and in another different place a day later, often while in full bloom - really the worst time to be transplanted - but if Mr Alfred willed it, then it was done.

Alfred's taste was supposed to be impeccable but in his country house he must have been influenced by visions of

DESPITE ITS SIZE THE HOUSE APPEARS TO HAVE TAKEN ONLY ABOUT 3 YEARS TO BUILD AND EMPLOYED A VERITABLE ARMY OF WORKMEN. IT WAS FINISHED IN JULY 1883...

An early photograph of the rear of the house, records work in progress. In the background, part of the house is still in scaffolding, with the staff ceremonially lined up on the terrace.

grandeur and perhaps a touch of rivalry with his brother-in-law Ferdinand, a member of the Viennese Branch of the Rothschild Family, who had married Alfred's sister, Evelina. Though she died tragically early in the marriage, Ferdinand made his home in England and eventually started building Waddesdon Manor around 1875.

Indeed, Ferdinand's bachelors' quarters were completed in 1880, about the time Alfred was starting work on Halton.

Waddesdon was chiefly based on sixteenth-century French Chateaux but Halton was a glorious mix of styles. The Victorians could range through history and the expanding world around them for ideas, and frequently did so, as well

as adding their own unique contribution and flavour. However, their more practical nature demanded that anything costly should show it. The result was a great mansion with roofs in the grand French manner - Alfred had requested a French chateau modelled on modern English lines, but it also incorporated touches of Italian Palaces as well as elements drawn from Scottish, classical and eastern architecture. Cecil Beaton nicknames this the Rothschild 'Grand French manner' but Mark Girouard notes that Halton was 'the last of the big French country houses'.

Whatever a visitor's reaction, Halton House cannot be ignored. Its luxury and elaboration has attracted compliments, awe, criticism and ridicule.

Algernon West described it as "an exaggerated nightmare of gorgeousness and senseless and ill-applied magnificence . . ." Later he modified this opinion, when he was forced to admit, somewhat grudgingly that: "lighted up and full of well-dressed people, it appeared quite tolerable".

Eustace Balfour said of it: "I have seldom see anything more terribly vulgar, outside it is a combination of a French Chateau and a gambling house. Inside it is badly planned, gaudily decorated . . . but the hideousness of everything, the showiness, the sense of lavish wealth thrust up your nose; the course mouldings, the heavy gilding always in the wrong place, the colour of the silk hangings! Eye hath not seen nor pen can write the ghastly coarseness of the sight".

Cecil Roth in a more restrained mood considers it is "an absurdly luxurious house commanding glorious views of the Vale of Aylesbury".

Morton comments dryly that it "was a vast pile of the most expensive ornamentation hundreds of thousands of pounds sterling could buy. It clashed luridly with simple glory of the Buckinghamshire beeches around it, exciting outrage and just possibly envy among various sensibilities".

Lionel de Rothschild passes it off as a house "looking like a huge wedding cake".

Even such a close and affectionate cousin as **Lady Battersea** cautiously ventures that the "approach might have been more advantageously laid out".

Mark Girouard, an authority on Victorian Country Houses, on the other hand, writing in our own day about these Victorian mansions, calls it "splendidly Louis Seize with another sumptuous winter garden . . . a notable tour de force of Rothschild extravagance".

Others, however, were completely bowled over by its size or impressed by its decoration. So what was it really like, to attract such varied reactions?

Exterior

The mansion is orientated with the front entrance looking south-east towards the hills and the back looking north-west towards the fountain. It is of brick, faced with white sandstone which has now mellowed to a pleasant golden colour. Parts of the roof are leaded, the rest being covered with grey-green Welsh slates. The terraces are finished in black and white marble.

The house has four floors with bays, balconies and turrets. There is a large well-lit basement, the land around being sufficiently held back by a retaining wall to allow a wide passageway often crossed by miniature bridges to the main house.

Decorative carvings of fruit, flowers and female heads abound upon the exterior walls of the house and porch, even in such places high above the entrance where viewing is difficult. A rounder of seasonal food welcomes staff to the service entrance and everywhere can be seen the AR monogram.

Porch

Typical of its era is the porch of the house. Outside the heavy entrance doors of glass and wood, is an arch surmounted with a small glass dome. Its two sides contain huge glass panels which enclose and give light to the entrance steps. Beyond, is an extension called the porte cochere - open at three sides and wide enough to allow the coach or carriage of a visitor to shelter beneath, so that its occupant could emerge unruffled, whatever the weather outside.

The side arches of the porch are decorated with carvings of maidens of the four seasons, while in the centre, angels of sun and moon extend their

The Porte Cochere

protection over all who pass beneath. A continuous freize extends along the whole ground floor front of the house.

Apart from a decorative and ubiquitous marigold, found everywhere inside and outside the house, it contains various symbols associated with the Rothschild coat of arms, granted in 1822 by the Austrian Empire and confirmed to the English branch of the family in 1838 by English Royal licence.

Thus various squares contain: the Lion of Hesse, an Imperial Austrian Eagle, triple Austrian ostrich feathers, a silver

North Entrance

Builders at Halton House

unicorn for peace, buffalo horns encircling a sixpointed star - probably originating from the Jewish horns of the altar and the Star of David, and finally the five arrows, their tips pointing downwards, symbolising the original five sons of their founding father.

Carved under some of the symbols are the works "Concordia Integritas Industria". Ironically, the new crest granted to Nathan de Rothschild, on being made an English Peer, was not given until 1885, two years after the house was completed.

Alfred was fond of using the Rothschild symbols. However, inside the mansion he mainly confines himself to his monogram AR and five arrows, which occasionally he changed to three, as a compliment to himself, as he was one of three Rothschild brothers. These signs appear in most rooms, on handles, finger plates, fire-stones, ceilings and decorative plaster work, from lintels to door panels, balconies to stairways.

Chimneys

Another feature Alfred appeared to have a weakness for is chimneys though in fairness to him this could have been a foible of the builder. They sprout in abundance from the house singly and in clusters, by various devices seeming to rise from the same level and all ending neatly evened off at the same height. Perhaps having endured the icy draughts of the imposing but uncomfortable large houses in his youth, Alfred was determined to have heat everywhere and share this benefit with everyone.

Belvedere

A description of the house would not be complete without a comment on the belvedere, the strange, dome-shaped, circular tower on the roof large enough to hold a dozen people, lapped in metal carrying the signatures of many former visitors and open to the winds of heaven. From this eminence, legend relates, messages could be passed from Rothschild house to Rothschild house across the Vale of Aylesbury. Not today however! Full grown trees obscure most of the view. Domes had long been in fashion when Alfred built, but his has survived, despite the odd lightning strike which bends the rod on its peak.

Interior Construction

The house itself incorporated some of the most modern ideas of Victorian high technology. It was of solid construction, the inside walls being of brick, several feet in thickness. The floors incorporated wrought iron beams to give them strength and make them fireproof - an important feature to owners of the late nineteenth century.

Water

A hydraulic lift transported luggage and fuel. This was powered by water stored in tanks high on the hill, neatly hidden by the roof of a decorative Swiss Chalet built especially to house them. A pumping station below drove the water uphill to the chalet, and the overflow, when required, filled an artificial lake in the grounds, which in winter doubled as a skating rink.

Water was used everywhere. Nothing was wasted, from the garden pools and grotto, the fountain and the greenhouses, to tanks in the turrets supplying the basement boilers, which in turn fed the hot water pipes supplying each floor of the house with plenty of heat or hot water. Ahead of their time, all water pipes were internal to prevent freezing in winter. There was even a cold plunge in the basement of the house - predating the sauna of today.

Lift Shaft

The Bucks Herald

Glass

Another notable feature of the house was its glass. Its windows were of the casement variety, with huge panels often opening onto a terrace or balcony as French doors. Wooden folding shutters were built into the thickness of the walls, often with highly decorated panels to the interior, and always with strong metal bars to secure them.

Yet more glass was used inside the house. Possibly influenced by the ideas of Paxton and the house at Mentmore, Alfred incorporated numerous glass domes, two for salon and staircase, one above the coach entrance, eleven in and around the winter garden and many modified ones for lighting corridors and giving ventilation in the service wing. Additional use of internal glass was made too, as in the great sliding door filling the arch between the Winter Garden and the Ante Room to both Drawing rooms, whose huge and heavy glass is still unblemished after over a century.

Mirrors were also incorporated prolifically as a form of decoration, often giving depth to an arch, even in such large areas as the salon, staircase and gallery. There is a touch of Versailles about the plenitude of mirrors in all the main rooms.

The Salon Dome

It is noticeable that the salon, the main hall in the heart of the house, about 1389 square feet and totally enclosed, with no outside windows save the enormous dome above, can still give the illusion of being one of the lightest rooms in the mansion. This is partly because of the clever manipulation of mirror and glass. Alfred loved light and ensured it was everywhere in his house.

Central Heating

There were many other inventions or innovations introduced into Alfred's new house. It contained the latest in up-to-date central heating. A ducted, warm-air system was installed for use on the ground floor. It worked with the ventilation shafts, which drew cold air into the house, warmed it in six heating chambers deep in the basement walls and then distributed it, through the grilles at the base of the walls, to all the main rooms and the winter garden, which had its own additional boilers and tanks. To ensure maximum comfort, most rooms also enjoyed large open fireplaces, the central salon having two. Radiators on other floors of the house - highly decorated as can be seen with those still surviving in situ - supplemented further deficiencies.

Sanitation

Sanitation was another luxury provided at Halton House, to a degree as high, or higher than that found in the homes of most contemporaries. There were ample toilets and a fair number of bathrooms. However, in the late nineteenth century many individuals, even among the richest and most up-to-date, still sat by flickering firelight in a hip bath, filled with water from hot and cold brass cans brought up by maids, a third can being used to pour on more hot water when the water cooled. Finally came the ritual of drying with a fluffy bath towel warming by the fire. It is, therefore not surprising that many bathrooms in Alfred's mansion still contained hip baths and only a few 'modern baths'. The greater surprise, however, is in finding a large iron bath for the servants, still preserved in the basement. Another uncommon feature was wash-handbasins, of which Halton had a few. Indeed, to safeguard health, the house had its own sewerage plant in a copse nearby.

Electricity, Gas and Railway

Halton House is one of the earliest to be lit with the then new electricity. Cragside is credited in 1880 with being the first home with all electric lighting. Alfred de Rothschild, however, apparently hedged his bets and used gas and electric. Well-labelled pipes in the basement - this seems a Rothschild idiosyncracy - attest to there being a gaselier in the central hall and a Sun Burner on the staircase, but old electric switches preserved on the ground floor refer to Electroliers in tiers - possibly connected with the five-tier winter garden chandeliers - and arc lamps on the roof, while basement plans of the original house show an accumulator room and an electricians' workshop. The central chandelier in the salon was changed a minimum of twice in the life of the house. Certainly, many of the upper bedrooms were lit with open gas jets, as extant fittings prove.

A plentiful supply of gas was ensured by Alfred, who owned the Gas Works in the village, bringing the gas up to the house and producing as a by-product, coke, which fired some of the house boilers used for gas, coke and open fires.

Thus, the ventilation, heating, lighting and water systems at Halton House were some of the most versatile and comprehensive of their era.

Coal was transported directly by road by Coal Merchants at Wendover Station Yard, the Station being on the Metropolitan and Great Central Joint Railway. A common misapprehension is to credit Alfred with the two minor (but busy) branch railway lines, from Wendover Station, which appeared on his estate as late as the First World War. They were not really his.

The first came early in the War to take the trees from Alfred's woodlands, felled and sawn into timbers from the trenches, on a special narrow gauge Jubilee line.

The second, built in 1917, was to supply the needs of the huge, sprawling Army Camp, by then established on Alfred's land.

CHAPTER 5

Charles Stephens, Shepherd

HALTON ESTATE

"Smile at us, pay us, pass us but do not quite forget". Chesterton

T he Estate that Alfred Charles de Rothschild inherited covered 1,400 acres and extended out to Aston Clinton, Weston Turville and Wendover, including Halton Village and numerous farms. In 1879, it was costing £134,509 to maintain. Alfred expanded it still further by purchase during his lifetime, until it contained 57 cottages, including those occupied by gamekeepers, servants and others, nine farms, together with fields, woodlands and coverts - in all totalling about 3,250 acres. Many purchases were made to consolidate holdings and to extend hunting rights over adjacent lands - presumably mainly for the benefit of his guests. However, it was the fashion of the time, so ever the perfect host - Alfred enabled his guests to conform.

Agents

His Halton estates were, however, more than a rich man's fancy. They were efficiently managed by his agent or land steward from his office in a room at Halton House. Sales from the estate and its farms included those of timber, cattle, bulls, heifers and sheep fleeces, grain, hay

His Halton estates were, however, more than a rich man's fancy. They were efficiently managed by his agent or land steward from his office in a room at Halton House.

and potatoes. They usually paid their way, despite high household expenses and their master's generosity to village and tenantry.

His first agent was Mr Swanston 1880-1898, followed by Mr Hubbard 1898-1918. In Alfred's employ from the time he was quite a young man, Mr John Swanston was still only 28 when he took over the responsibility of being Alfred's Halton agent in 1880. During the months of his last illness the man who was to replace him appears to have taken over the reins increasingly, up to the time of Mr Swanston's death in midsummer 1898 at the early age of 46.

Mr Frederick Joseph Hubbard was 54 when he took over from Mr Swanston, being older at the start of his employment than Mr Swanston at the end. His son, Jack, became quite a favourite of Alfred. Mr Hubbard continued as agent at Halton until Alfred's death, although in the latter years he appears to have been much helped by his son. He was the main contact between the rarely seen Mr Alfred de Rothschild and those employed in his house and grounds, together with their families and the whole local area.

Many of Alfred's good works and

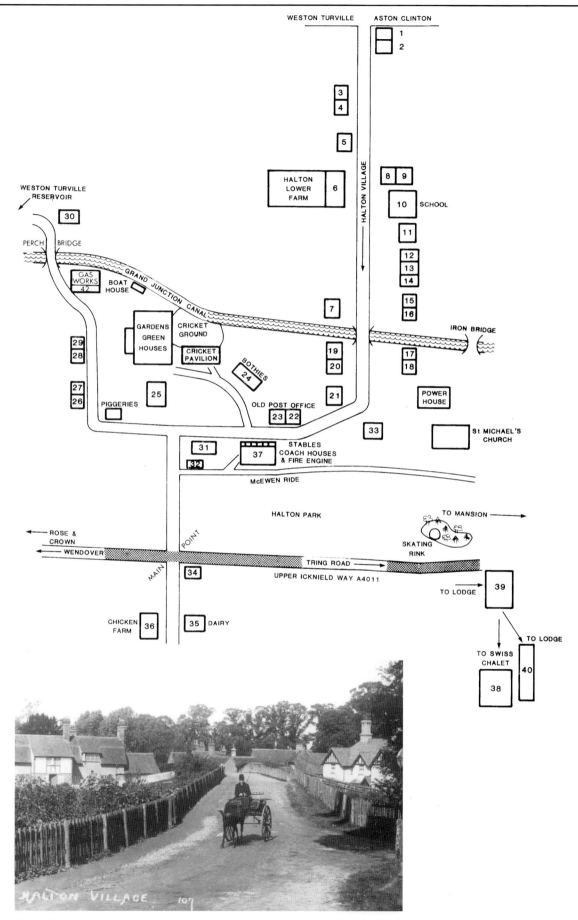

WESTON TURVILLE

ASTON CLINTON

1
2

3
4

5

HALTON
LOWER
FARM

6

HALTON VILLAGE

8 9

10 SCHOOL

11

12
13
14

15
16

WESTON TURVILLE
RESERVOIR

30

PERCH BRIDGE

GRAND JUNCTION CANAL

GAS
WORKS
42

BOAT
HOUSE

7

IRON BRIDGE

GARDENS
GREEN
HOUSES

CRICKET
GROUND

CRICKET
PAVILION

29
28

27
26

PIGGERIES

25

BOTHIES
24

19
20

17
18

21

POWER
HOUSE

OLD POST OFFICE

23 22

33

St MICHAEL'S
CHURCH

31

32

37

STABLES
COACH HOUSES
& FIRE ENGINE

McEWEN RIDE

HALTON PARK

TO MANSION

ROSE &
CROWN

POINT

SKATING
RINK

WENDOVER

MAIN

34

TRING ROAD

UPPER ICKNIELD WAY A4011

TO LODGE

39

TO LODGE

CHICKEN
FARM

36

35 DAIRY

TO SWISS
CHALET

38

40

Halton Village

Lodge Gates   *Post Office*

	Occupier	Employment	Place Name	At Present
	Occupier	Employment	Place Name	At Present
1.	Mr Drake	Gamekeeper	Bye Green	Privately owned
2.	Mr Richard	Buildings	Bye Green	Privately owned
3.	Mr Walter Warner*	Farm Poultry	The Barracks	Demolished
4.		Farm Poultry	The Barracks	Demolished
5.	Mr Fred Gee	Head Gamekeeper	The Kennels	Demolished
6.	Mr Jack Hubbard	Assistant Agent	Halton Lower Farm	Converted to several private dwellings
7.	Mr Bubb	Gardener	Canal Cottages	Converted to single private dwelling
8.	Mr Joe & Alfred Gomm	Farm Workers		Demolished, replaced by by OAP council flats
9.	Mr Jack Nash	Farm Worker		" "
10.	Miss Amy Peake	Teacher	School House	Privately Owned
11.	Mr Joe Ginger	Groom		" "
12.	Mr Tom Ginger & Mr Morris	Grooms		" "
13.		Security Police		" "
14.	Mr Zenthon	Security Police		" "
15.	Mr Slade	Kitchen Hand		" "
16.	Mr Wyatt	Kitchen Hand		" "
17.	Mr Sharp	Farm Worker		Converted to single dwelling
18.	Mr Alfred Norwood	Power House		
19.	Mr Thirtle	Gardener	Brookside	
20.	Mr Stevens	Gardener	Brookside	Demolished & replaced by OAP council flats
21.	Mr Heels	Game Keeper (Son, George worked at mansion)		
22.	Mr Joe Warner*	Farm & Poultry		Privately Owned
23.	Mr Sharp	PO & Shop - not in Rothschild employ		Converted to private dwelling
24.	Mr Cryer, Strike, etc (Single men)	Gardeners	Bothy	
25.	Mr Sanders	Head Gardener	Garden House	
26.	Mr George Warner*	Estate Worker		Privately Owned
27.	Mr Towersey	Head Chauffeur		Privately Owned
28.	Mr Frederick Day	Electrical Engineer	Power House	
29.	Mr Albert Leslie Coe	Butler		
30.	Mr Franz Paine	Gamekeeper	The Perch	
31.	Mr Frederick Hubbard	Agent	The Grange	Former CO's residence. Then 2nd officers' Mess. Demolished
32.	Mr Dade	Security Police	St Michael's Lodge	Halton Cottage Privately owned
33.	Mr Trodd	Butler	Ivy Cottage	" "
34.		Keeper	Beacon Hill Cottage	House at Main Point - MOD Families quarter
35.		Dairy	Beacon Hill House	Officer Commanding RAF Halton's Residence
36.			Beacon Hill Poultry Farm	Stables for RAF Halton and Riding for the Disabled
37.	Mr George Budd	Head Coachman	Grange Yard Stables	Converted to private dwelling
38.	Mrs Vince	Housekeeper Chalet	Swiss Chalet	Privately owned
39.	Mr Walker	Security Police	Mansion Hill Lodge	" "
40.	Mr George Pope	Gamekeeper	Aston Hill Lodge	" "
41.	Mr Jack Hicks	Gamekeeper	Peacock Lodge	" "
42.	Mr Beesom		Gas Works' House	" "

VIEW IN HALTON GARDENS.

Agricultural Show at the Ornamental Lake.

projects must have stemmed from the comprehensive mind of Mr Hubbard. In any case it was he who carried decisions into action. His well-known figure was often seen riding around the Estate first on horseback, and later when he began to suffer badly from gout, in a carriage. There were mixed feelings as to how well-liked he was by those who served Alfred. There is little doubt as to his

efficiency - the estate prospered under his control. Reports, however, on his latter years say that his temper was often bad, and "if he could put a spoke in anyone's wheel he would". Parents often invoked his name as a threat to misbehaving children but there is little doubt that he kept good order in Alfred's Halton Estate, and was extremely well paid at £75 a quarter before Alfred died.

Carpenters

Alfred's Tenants

To his tenants Alfred was an extremely generous landlord and the local area benefited from his good works. It also drew much of its employment and business from the estate.

Part of Halton Village was rebuilt for the estate workers and those houses and cottages bear the unmistakable stamp of Rothschild, being decorated with plaster panels of country crafts, rural scenes or the Rothschild ostrich-feather badge. They were well maintained, as Alfred liked to see tidy cottages and gardens as he passed from his train at the railway station to the mansion. Tenants were supplied with free flowers to plant in their front gardens, though they could grow what they liked behind their homes. Children, however, were preferred to be unseen and unheard, and many remember being removed from their games and hushed when it was known that Mr Alfred would come riding by.

Halton Agricultural Show

In the 1900s the Local Chiltern Hills'

Agricultural Association was allowed to hold its annual show in the grounds of Halton House. This was a great day for visitors, villagers, staff and local folk alike. Best suits, fashionable dresses and elaborate bonnets vied with the colour and variety of the exhibits.

Sightseers crowded the many marquees, admiring the size of the vegetables and beauty of the flowers from Halton hot-houses or private gardens. After examining these, families could cool themselves beside Alfred's lake, listen at the bandstand to music selections from Alfred's private orchestra or visit the tents dispensing free food and drinks to all the guests. Families met to exchange the latest news and if they were lucky they might even catch sight of their usually unseen benefactor, doffing his hat to their greetings, his face wreathed in smiles, hugely delighted with the success of the show. Then came the solemn judging, the prizes, the celebrations or consolations, and dancing or drinking the night out. Later came reflection and the pleasant prospect of looking forward to another show next year.

Mr Frederick Hubbard

Village School

Alfred's generosity did not stop there. Though unlike his family and contemporaries in many ways, he shared their enthusiasm for learning and actively encouraged it. At Halton, he built a large reading room and kept it supplied with daily newspapers and magazines for the use of the villagers. He also built a village school and provided a schoolmistress, Miss Summer, whom he paid and later pensioned, when on her retirement she was replaced by a younger person, Miss Amy Peake.

As most of the pupils were drawn from his estate, he took a personal interest in the children, demanding to be informed of every birthday and ordering a birthday present for each child. This was supplemented by presents of money, which usually accompanied Alfred's Halton visits or a special celebration, as well as a regular shilling at Christmas. He supplied new school outfits for the pupils, contributed to the School Clothing Club, and paid for a Christmas tree, parties, treats, and school outings. Children were taught useful skills in addition to the normal curriculum and usually followed their parents into employment on the estate when they left school

Alfred's interest additionally extended to the Wendover School since some of its pupils came from his estate, and he also gave them some financial help.

Head Gardener's Cottage

The first page of Halton House Visitors' Book. The first entry is Albert Edward, the Prince of Wales

FIRST VISITORS

"I have already sent you several letters to say that everything has gone off so far perfectly at Halton. I now take up my pen to send you a few details."

16 Jan '84 Leopold de Rothschild

In July of 1883 Halton House was completed. There it stood, shining in all its pristine newness, white against the blue summer sky. Then came the decorators, the upholsterers, the furnishers, and the carters with their crates of precious paintings and valuable objects.

However, though standing ready for its owner, the house did not receive its first Royal Visitor until the following year.

Leopold of Ascott House, Alfred's brother, says "I hear that all the country people are looking forward to Alfred's Ball with the greatest delight and the inhabitants of Tring are busy decorating the small town."

On Tuesday 15 January 1884 the long anticipated visit took place. It was evening and everything was in readiness. Promptly at six, Alfred left the house in a brougham and pair. At quarter-to-seven he was at Tring station greeting his Royal Highness, Albert, Prince of Wales, as he stepped off the special Euston train, having arrived early after a journey of just under thirty-five minutes - no mean achievement even in these days. This was particularly so, in view of the slight delay caused by the discovery of some sticks of dynamite on the line at Primrose Hill. As

LEOPOLD DE ROTHSCHILD, ARRIVING ON THE SAME TRAIN FROM HIS WORK AT THE BANK, ESCORTED THE TWO PRINCES AND EARL GRANVILLE TO HALTON IN AN OPEN LANDAU.

no fuses or detonators were found, it was comfortingly deduced that there was no malicious intent. "After all", one reporter commented "we live in violent times!" The Prince of Wales was accompanied in the Salon coach by the Prince of Saxe-Coburg Gotha.

Among the royal party in other compartments were Earl Granville, the Duchess of Manchester (a Royal favourite), the Marquess of Hartington, Sir Henry Drummond Wolff, Sir Arthur Sullivan, Sir Henry Colcroft, and Lady Mandeville.

Unfortunately, Lady Greville, also invited, was ill and Lord and Lady Beresford could not come that day, having to nurse a sick child. Leopold de Rothschild, arriving on the same train from his work at the bank, escorted the two Princes and Earl Granville to Halton in an open landau.

Tring was 'en fete' to greet its Royal guest. Deprived of providing the usual guard of honour, because this was a private visit, the town had elected a local committee to see that nothing else was lacking. The usually quiet little town was flooded with crowds, causing the Police Superintendent to warn the public to beware of the 'light-fingered gentry.'

Edward, Prince of Wales and Alfred at Waddesdon Manor

On entering the town one of the first things to meet the Prince's eyes was a triumphal arch, inscribed with the word 'Welcome'. The town hoped that the message "Vivat Regina" on the reverse, would be conveyed directly by the Prince to his mother, since it was the last message he would see on departing. Under the arch and down a street lined with poles, entwined with evergreens and dotted with coloured lamps, the Prince drove on towards another arch, this time carrying the slogans, "Long Life and Peace" and "God Bless the Prince of Wales".

At the entrance to Tring Park, home of Sir Nathaniel de Rothschild, Member of Parliament and Alfred's elder brother, the Prince saw further elaborate decorations, particularly on the house of Sir Nathaniel's agent, Mr Parkes, whose ivy walls were scattered with shields and flags and whose every window was glowing with a myriad of candles. Everywhere houses and shops were plentifully decorated with bunting and flags, gas and oil lamps, among which the unusual masonic touches of Mr Knight, the local plumber, especially caught the eye.

Side roads also contributed light and colour to the town. As the procession of coaches moved up the High Street to Meads Hill, it encountered a third triumphal arch, which proclaimed "Health and Happiness" and "God Save the Queen". Nearby, the post office sparkled with oil lamps of different colours and beyond, leading into Western Road, Venetian masts carried strings of flags criss-crossing the street.

These continued right up to the Britannia Inn, where the last arch stood, covered in evergreens and embellished in the centre with the Prince of Wales' Feathers, the flags of France and Turkey on either corner. Below was the motto "A Loyal People Greet Thee" and on the other side, seen on leaving, "God Speed Thy Way". From here to just below the New Inn, itself sporting a huge ensign on a high mast, the way was lined with large oil lamps fastened to telegraph poles.

Leopold notes: "The little town of Tring was quite gay with Venetian Masts, triumphal arches, flowers, banners and lights but what was far more noteworthy was a happy crowd of country people cheering and shouting. The Prince of Wales seemed pleased at this enthusiastic welcome".

The piece de resistance, however, was yet to come. There were still some miles of countryside to be covered between Tring and Halton House, and this was lit along its whole length with flaming torches and chinese lanterns held by 240 men and boys, lending an almost fairytale atmosphere to the scene.

As the guests drove into the grounds of Halton House they passed into a new era of electricity, for, by the aid of twelve enormous electric roof-mounted lamps, the towers of the house, the gardens, the statuary and the mansion itself were dramatically revealed. Even the fountain played its part, throwing up coloured jets of water higher than the trees encircling it. The display was normally intended to represent the Rothschild plumes, but on such an occasion, it could conveniently double for the Prince of Wales' feathers.

Alfred, whose carriage followed the Prince's, was quickly afoot under the

porte cochere in front of the house, ready to welcome the Prince to the wonders of his new home. The guests then dispersed to make ready for their meal as it was nearly eight o'clock.

Special flowers had been brought from London by the firm of Veitch's, who regularly supplied Alfred's needs and whose artist, Mr Archer, was in charge of the decorations everywhere. At Alfred's particular insistence, no guest at his table must dodge masses of greenery to be seen and heard by the diner opposite, as frequently happened

Tring decorated on 15 January 1884. Everywhere houses and shops were plentifully decorated with bunting and flags, gas and oil lamps.

Dinner was served in Alfred's new dining room; Trodd the Butler presides on the left

elsewhere. To this end, Mr Archer could be seen earlier that evening, checking the height and width of all the arrangements with a ruler and levelling any offending flower.

Dinner was served in Alfred's new dining room, overlooked by Reynold's large portrait of Lady Bamfylde, which was much admired. The meal went off without a hitch, the menu painstakingly selected by Alfred and approved by his mother, whose advice Alfred sought over many details of his houseparty.

Food was brought from the new kitchens to the serving room, where each course was reheated before the footmen carried it out and laid it on the table. It was then served the English way, guests' plates being taken by footmen to the serving dish, while glasses were filled by the Butler, who remained at the sideboard, dispensing wine to the footmen serving the guests.

During the meal it was noticeable that, though encouraging his guests' appetite, Alfred ate and drank sparingly. The table conversation,

however, was both sprightly and witty, a style much cultivated by Alfred, who ensured that everyone was included. Not surprisingly, in such a convivial atmosphere, several of the guests lingered over their fruit at the end. Music was supplied by Jacoby's band, which was to become Alfred's resident orchestra. Leopold tells us that the band played exquisitely and he obviously spoke for others. Afterwards the party split up, some to play whist with the Prince of Wales and others to play poker, from which most had drifted off to bed by about two in the morning.

The next day about thirty guests were out shooting pheasants. Enthusiastic beaters, conscripted from the village, flushed out the birds and the shoot was carefully supervised by Alfred's 14 gamekeepers, smart in their brass-buttoned uniform of waistcoat and navy jacket in good Melton cloth, each lapel proudly displaying a brass 'A de R'. These were worn over light coloured breeches and topped by a black bowler hat. Perhaps to the relief of the lazier souls, the morning's activities started rather later than intended, owing to an early fog, but this cleared soon enough to enable the Prince to make a good bag, even though a forecast of 600 birds had been made and only 400 were, in fact, brought down.

That night the house party was joined by Alfred's cousins Constance and Cyril Flower from Aston Clinton together with their own guests, the men very grand in red coats. This time dinner was served to forty. An unusual silver basket of orchids on the table, a special present to Alfred, attracted admiring comments, as did the menu, the speedy service and the music. After dinner a conjurer, especially brought from Paris, entertained the guests. For one of his tricks he took a cigarette case out of a hat, presenting it to the Prince. A deft flick of the wrist and the plain gold case miraculously changed to another with the Prince's own monogram on it - yet another detail masterminded by Alfred in his concern to please his guests. The night ended much as the previous one, the visitors leaving at midnight, and the rest playing whist or poker until the early hours.

Despite Thursday, 17th January, being the day of the Grand Ball, many of the guests were early out with the hounds hunting in the morning. Even so, business could not be entirely forgotten with despatches and boxes arriving at all times. The evening saw the drive busy with carriages bringing local notables and titled families of the area to the Ball. This was their chance to satisfy their curiosity about the new house and its owner, now in their midst. The mansion was again flooded with electric light both inside and out and filled with the most brilliant decorations, people and music, as, with the Prince of Wales, Alfred played host to the county.

Emma Louise von Rothschild of Tring Park, who had dined just before the ball with Alfred's house guests, later described "this charming fete" to her aunt.

"The Prince was most kind, talkative and bright, pleased with everything, admired this house, thought Alfred's cook by far the best in London and was much puzzled by the dish called 'poussins' on the menu". This speciality called 'Poussins Haltonais' normally contained young out-of-season pheasants. Emma comments that "they might have been called 'torn poussins', they were so friable" . . .".

"The country people arrived before the gentlemen had left the dining room", where the excellent port launched them merrily on the incoming guests. "Someone asked us if the gentleman with a large ribbon (Sir Henry Drummond Wolff) was a distinguished foreigner, to which I replied he had been an envoy extraordinary. Sir Arthur Sullivan, who heard my reply, added sotto voce "Yes, very extraordinary". Dancing continued until half past three in the morning and vast quantities of champagne were consumed.

Despite this, on the Friday, the last day of the Prince's visit, "most of the house guests were down to breakfast at 10.30. The day was very clear and the view from the dining room provided a charming accompaniment to an excellent dejeuner".

In the evening, his carriage filled with hothouse fruit, flowers and gifts, which Alfred had showered upon him, the Prince returned along the same route to Tring railway station, cheering crowds lining the way.

Emma sums up the momentous week thus - "You must forgive me if I have not done justice to Alfred's entertainment. I feel that descriptions are generally imperfect, but I cannot conclude without saying that everyone was thoughtful, hospitable and genial kindness to his guests".

Another member of the family, Louise von Rothschild, later writes from Frankfurt with devastating understatement. "The festivities at Halton have gone off most successfully and Alfred must, I am sure, have been pleased when all was well over, for such entertainment must have given a great deal of trouble."

Thus ended what must have been certainly the most exciting, and possibly the most outstanding, house party that Alfred ever held at Halton House.

CHAPTER 7

The Domestic Staff at Halton

THE
SERVICE WING

"They also serve, who only stand and wait." Milton

After all the celebrations had finished, the distinguished guests had gone and Alfred was left to enjoy his house on his own, what decorations and furnishings met his eye? What was this marvellous mansion really like in its prime? First we must look at its historical context.

The Victorians inherited a growing industrial and agricultural revolution, with the accompanying mass production and specialisation so admired by the followers of the doctrine of Adam Smith. Attitudes formed in the factory percolated into the home and the more relaxed eighteenth-century household became more rigidly organized and sub-divided in the nineteenth.

Servants were not to be seen or heard, so special wings, corridors and staircases had to be added for them. There was a rigid hierarchy among guests, family and servants. Rules evolved, the breach of which could bring almost more social disgrace than lapses in morality. Money was the only palliative. Advances in medicine were reducing infant mortality but had not yet introduced family planning. A normal household might

THE MANSION COMPRISES TWO DIFFERENT AND DISTINCT AREAS - THE MAIN HOUSE WITH ITS ACCOMMODATION FOR MASTER AND GUESTS, AND THE SERVICE WING WHERE STAFF LIVED AND WORKED.

therefore hold perhaps a dozen offspring together with their attendants, as well as adults with their servants. These in turn required numerous and larger rooms, their high ceilings necessitated because of the noxious gases from the new gas lights.

These were among the factors affecting the Victorian Houses we see today, and Halton House, though built for a bachelor, conforms with many of these traditional features, as well as adding some peculiar to itself.

The mansion comprises two different and distinct areas - the main house with its accommodation for master and guests, and the service wing where staff lived and worked. In the main house there were four floors. The service wing took the form of a long low building to the east of the main building, where there were only two storeys and a basement.

THE BASEMENT

In "The Gentleman's House", written in 1864 by Robert Kerr, a planner of the period, domestic accommodation is decided into nine main sections. Halton conforms to this pattern in all except the laundry. The remaining eight are: kitchen,

*North exterior showing
winter garden (right)
and service wing (left).*

SERVICE WING BASEMENT PLAN

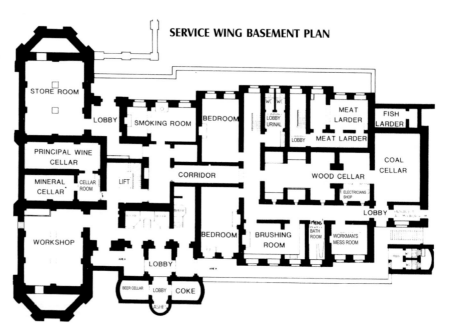

the south front, but both took adequate light and air from the wide passage encircling the Service Wing of the house.

Toilets

There were three groups of toilets for staff as well as private ones for such people as the male cook. There were also several sinks - a feature unusual in houses of this period.

Two internal staircases were provided near the toilets for men, together with another emerging behind the baize doors to the main house and common to all. An external stairway leading down to a back door and further toilets served the needs of workmen, outdoor staff and tradesmen.

Rooms

Room designations differed from time to time but the overall picture remains remarkably stable. Male staff in junior positions were divided into workmen and men, each having their own mess rooms with the additon of a smoking room. The Head Cook (male) originally had a bedroom downstairs with a toilet and fireplace - it still today contains a very ancient radiator and there was another bedroom opposite. Later this room became a staff room.

Elsewhere were wine cellars for the master and beer for the staff, together with ample room for keeping fuel indoors - coal, coke and wood. Meat was stored at the back of the house in well-aired larders with an adjacent sink, and behind the wall cutting these off, was located the Fish Larder. Below ground, with no doors or windows, this larder was accessible only from above, and served as an ice house in days before deep freezers. Here ice was stored and fish kept fresh. From this room emanated such specialities as the salmon-in-ice, served to Nasr-ed-Din, Shah of Persia. In today's house this is a lost room, the trapdoor being cemented over.

Additionally the household carpenters were equipped with a workshop downstairs. A further range of rooms used mainly by the footmen also appeared here: a brushing room for

common rooms for upper servants, common rooms for lower servants, bakery, cellar, storage, servants' private rooms, supplementaries and thorough-fares.

As Halton House was so wide, rooms in the basement were laid out rather like those in the plan of a ship. The outer rooms were mainly for staff and the inner ones for the storage of coal, coke, wood, wine, minerals, boilers etc. Everywhere walls were covered with whiteglazed tiles for the purposes of hygiene. Pipes for gas and water ran along the barrel-vaulted brick ceilings, each being painted clearly with its function and area, such as "Water pipes to servants' toilets, sinks and baths".

Windows on the north (fountain) side were generally set higher than those in clothes and shoes; a lamp room for filling and trimming oil lamps, which together with gas lights were still used in the upper rooms of the house, and a knife room for cleaning silver pieces and cutlery with jeweller's rouge and chamois leather.

Laundry

Many houses provided a series of rooms and yards for the laundry in the service wing but this was missing at Halton House. It is obvious that Mr Alfred preferred to relegate clothes lines of unmentionables blowing in the breeze, to the village, where a special white-tiled laundry was built. This arrangement may also have had something to do with the architectural plan here, where the basement was male territory, as men predominated in a staff of whom the master, in any case, was a bachelor. Females, fewer in number than usual, were kept firmly above stairs.

Dairy

Alfred's Dairy was also removed some distance from the house. It was, in fact, situated at Beacon Hill, where those staff employed there could also live. It was, therefore, equipped with a bedroom, drawing room, and sitting room, in addition to the usual dairy rooms. Again this was the preserve of the female staff, who were thus kept away from the Mansion.

THE GROUND FLOOR

In Victorian days there was a well-defined organisation of staff into various departments under their own particular head. House planners endeavoured, as far as possible, to group together the rooms associated with these sections, as found at Halton.

Heading the Halton Indoor staff were the Butler, the Housekeeper and the Chief Cook, while the Head Coachman, plus later the Chief Chauffeur, and the Head Gardener, presided outside. The Steward's sphere of authority lay as much outside the house as inside.

The Steward controlled the whole of the estate and was sometimes called the agent or bailiff. His room, near the luggage entrance, enabled him to receive visitors and conduct business without disturbing the rest of the house. In later years his room was moved to the gallery above stairs. Much of his daily work required him to go out and about, but technically he was in charge of all the staff both indoor and outdoor. His role had evolved over the centuries until his main preoccupation lay in deputising for the owner and dealing with all finances and business concerning the estate and its lands. When a Steward was still employed in the house, the heads of staff would dine with him, but when, as here, he was frequently out on estate business, the privilege of head of staff usually fell to the Butler or Housekeeper. They were

SERVICE WING GROUND FLOOR PLAN

waited on by the duty footman and usually dined before Mr Alfred.

The Butler, assisted at Halton by an under-butler, enjoyed his own room called the butler's pantry. Later again this became the pantry sitting room for the Butler and his staff. It was lined with cupboards and contained a sink, a table and a comfortable armchair beside the fire. Footmen and indoor servants were in the Butler's charge, while wines, silver and table linen were his special care. Under his eye was the safe or plate closet - a locked room fitted with beautiful airtight, red mahogany doors and drawers - where at night he or a footman slept close at hand. Nearby was the serving room with sink, hot plate and all necessary for the smooth serving of the dining room meals, in which Alfred took such pride and where the Butler deployed his staff of footmen.

Kerr recommends the best positioning of the butler's pantry as: "near as possible, indeed close to the dining room for the convenience of service. It ought to be removed from the general traffic and especially from the back door for the safety of the plate. The communication with the Wine and beer cellars must be

ready and in a manner private . . . (it also) ought to overlook the Approach so that timely notice may be had of the arrival of a carriage."

Since Halton was so large, no single room could fulfil all these criteria but by its positioning in this house, Alfred indicates his scale of priorities. Control of the dining room was pre-eminent. In order to achieve this, Kerr's last function was delegated to the Steward or Under-Butler.

The Housekeeper's room faced south. With its fireplace and toilet 'en suite', lined with cupboards for china and

Footmen with Trodd, the Butler, top right. Another footman carries Alfred's white poodle.

Chef and two female cooks, called Annie and Frances, in the kitchen

Chauffeurs and 5 cars in kitchen yard with spiked walls. Centre car is a Zedel Phaeton (open) with Renaults on either side. An Elswick is far right and Wolseley far left. All have early Buckinghamshire registrations.

household linen, it must have provided a pleasant sitting room for an older lady. Her main concern was the day-to-day cleanliness and comfort of all accommodation particularly the bedrooms of Mr Alfred and his guests, paying particular attention to the requirements of lady visitors. Indeed, most female matters were her province including the discipline and well-being of all female staff both outside and inside the house, especially the housemaids.

Beside her room were the still room, the store room and the maids' sitting room, with the staircase leading to their bedroom between. The name of the still room had a long and ancient history going back to the time when a housewife distilled essences and prepared herbs for luxury use or the treatment of household ills. In the 1880s it was the room where the housekeeper found the items dear to the newly-acquired habit of afternoon tea. Here and in the next door store, she kept preserves, sugar, coffee, tea and biscuits and the delicious cakes, which sometimes found their way into boxes stowed away in the carriages of departing guests.

The Chief Cook was head of the kitchen, in former centuries a male preserve but now admitting women, often in the lowly tasks of preparing vegetables and washing up. Alfred

employed an extremely large kitchen staff but in view of his noted reputation as a gastronome, this is hardly surprising. The Chief Cook was a Frenchman, a culinary artist.

He presided over several speciality cooks, one who was famous for the most superb pastry and another who excelled in sweets and confectionery decoration. Both had a special room set aside for their work. There were, however, only two female cooks among the rest of the male staff who prepared, cooked and washed up, so that the kitchen often employed up to fifteen persons - ten 'hands' and five cooks and sometimes more if Alfred were entertaining a particularly large number of guests.

The kitchen was extremely large, fitted with the latest cooking stoves and equipment - no open fireplaces here, as in other less up-to-date houses - and dominated by a huge wooden table for food preparation. Twelve feet above them was a louvred roof for expelling steam and smells. There was also the usual corkscrew arrangement of corridors between kitchen and dining room, in case any stray smell of cooking dare to percolate into the sacred domain of the dining room.

Robert Kerr declares: "It becomes the foremost of all maxims, therefore, that the Servants' Department shall be separated from the main house, so that what passes on either side of the boundary shall both be invisible and inaudible to the other".

Behind the kitchen was the scullery for preparation of vegetables and washing up, with an exit for the vegetable store. On one side of this island of activity were miscellaneous larders, pantries, a dairy and access to the separate downstairs stores for fish and meat. Nearby, also, was an office for the Head Cook in his capacity as Manager and administrator in the little world of the kitchen staff, and this room eventually became a sitting room for all the male kitchen staff.

The Upper servants having their own private rooms, the servants' hall was the only common ground where most of the staff met. Lower servants in the hierarchy were the footmen and housemaids, as well as the grooms for the horses and later the mechanics for electric lights and cars. About a dozen carpenters and maintenance men were also employed about the house. All the members of staff ate in the servants' hall, often served by the odd job boy. Outside staff such as gardeners, keepers, foresters and estate workers ate in their own quarters elsewhere.

The Head Coachman presided over the stables outside. He was responsible for all the coaches and carriages kept for the house, the horses, which included the ponies and palominos later introduced by Alfred, and the large staff employed for their maintenance and service. He had nothing to do with the animals of the circus, which was organized separately. Mess rooms and sitting rooms were supplied with the harness rooms alongside.

When Alfred introduced cars to Halton, he appointed a Chief Chauffeur, who acquired a staff of four others. These co-existed with the stable staff, although becoming more important as the years passed and Alfred's preference for cars grew. Cars were painted in the distinctive Rothschild colours of blue with strips of yellow, in the same way as the decorations on the harnesses of the horses which also bore Alfred's distinctive monogram on their saddle cloths.

Mr Rolf was Head Chauffeur in Alfred's later years. He was evidently highly thought of by his master to the extent that he handled the payments and expenses of his little fleet, answerable only to the agent. By the time war broke out he was paying for government insurance stamps for the chauffeurs and licences and insurance on the cars. In his will, Alfred rewarded him with a small legacy of £500.

Bedrooms

The first and only bedroom floor of the Service Wing was cut off from the Main house with a roof between. It was shaped like a 'U' with its open end to the kitchen yard. Into the space in the middle projected the ventilated, glass roofs of the kitchen quarters, onto which faced the windows of the bedroom corridors. A wall separated the rooms of the men from the women and each part was served by a separate staircase.

There were four upstairs bedrooms for indoor male staff and two basement bedrooms, later discontinued when Alfred decided to introduce his swimming bath. Among those male bedrooms were those of the Footman, the Hall Boy and the Odd-Job Man.

SERVICE WING
FIRST FLOOR BEDROOMS

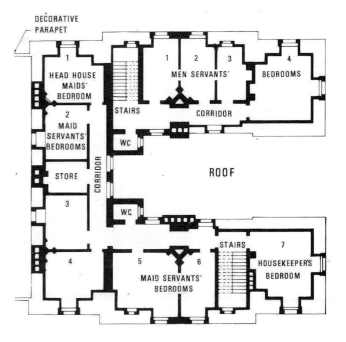

There were, on the other hand, seven bedrooms and a large store room allotted to the women, among whom were the Housekeeper and the Head Housemaid. Housemaids had to live-in, at least part of the time, since some of their duties were servicing the bedrooms in the main part of the house.

Each large staff bedroom, about 9½ feet high, equipped with a fireplace, gas light and outside window with shutters, was intended for the use of only one person. Most enjoyed a fine view across to the north or south garden trees.

It was expected that domestic staff stayed single. If any servant married then he or she faced three choices. If the master wished, he could allocate a nearby cottage or house which could be used for the individual to "live out", providing it in no way interfered with duty. Otherwise the spouse had to live apart and visit the partner as and when possible. The final option was to marry and give up employment - a stark choice when work was hard to find. Generally, Victorian households contained few married staff - marriage was definitely not encouraged.

Alfred, however unconventional in many ways, had no objection to servants marrying and staying in his employ, provided that it did not inconvenience him. Most of the houses on his estate were occupied by married staff and he exhibited great generosity and thought on gifts for weddings, as well as pensions and homes for retired servants, together with medical or hospital care for those who were sick.

Speaking tubes connected the servants' wing with the main house. These had a whistle hanging on them, used much as those on board ship to summon attention. The remnants of these tubes can still be found today on most floors of the house, in many cases preserving their original labels. The inevitable bells that replaced them and the master console, still in many Victorian houses, have been dismantled.

No communication between the bedrooms of the staff and of the main house was possible with a flat roof in between. Housemaids had to descend to the ground floor and use the main house

secondary staircases for access to their housemaid's closets on each floor, stacked high with linen and cleaning tools for the guest rooms they served. Today the service wing bedrooms have been joined to the main building and this area is now known as the Chinese Landing.

Staff

Staff below stairs, however, had a very high opinion of Alfred. He may have been a pernickety, eccentric and at times infuriating master but he was also unusually considerate, loyal and exceedingly generous. On few estates did a cart distribute hot coffee and bread and butter to all the outdoor staff at midmorning, or offer beer, bread and cheese to all callers in the kitchen.

Stories were also told of the sovereign paid to the gatekeeper who brushed the stones from the path when Mr Alfred's carriage passed and that this happened

Alfred entertains the local men of Halton during the celebration of Queen Victoria's Diamond Jubilee. There was a second sitting for the women

regularly, although both knew the truth of this little charade. Another story tells of Alfred's concern one day when a servant made a mistake in serving tea.

"She is tired", explained an embarrassed housekeeper. Alfred's eyebrows rose. Next day another maid was engaged to take over half the duties of the first. It was Alfred's pride that, as he had enough money, none of his staff should be overworked. Better too many staff than too much work!

In any case work was not too onerous when Mr Alfred was away though it continued in his long absences, being self-generating. On the few yearly occasions, however, when he was visiting, the house must have sprung to life as a veritable hive of industry, especially if it was known that he was accompanied by his usual house party. Then the staff worked with a will for the few days their master remained in residence. They were also well paid by the standards of the day, and would have

been paid more had other local employers not objected, because it would have caused their wage bills to rise. Alfred, therefore, partly found a way round this difficulty by paying higher rates to staff who accompanied him to London or elsewhere. The same generosity was found in the length of annual holidays.

His staff was, therefore, a happy well-knit and lively one, which could get up to mischief when not watched too closely, especially when licenced by such affairs as the Servants' Ball or other, not infrequent, festivities. Naturally Alfred paid but declined to be present.

Formal occasions, which fell at least once a year, called for big entertainments, marquees, bands and free drinks and a banquet for all staff, their families and many local visitors. These were great occasions - everyone in their Sunday best. Invitations were formal and sent out on beautifully coloured, gilt-edged cards, such as the one for the

63

The Halton Fire Brigade

Queen Victoria's Jubilee and the coronation celebrations of King Edward VII and King George V. Staff sometimes took photographs of "Mr Alfred" and later carried them into the trenches of World War I treasuring them alongside snaps of wives and sweethearts.

Consequently, Alfred was served with great loyalty. Most of his staff stayed with him throughout his life and were mentioned by name and well rewarded in his will. It was also remarked that he always spoke politely to them - preferring Christian names for the maidservants and treating maids like Duchesses and vice-versa. The men he called by surname - not unusual with friends in other walks of life.

Among names of household staff still preserved in photographs and records are his gigantic valet who escorted him everywhere, Frederick Hubbard, his Halton Agent and Jack Hubbard his son, Rolf his Head Chauffeur, Trodd and Coe his Butlers, his faithful barber Charles, Mrs Ferguson his Housekeeper, Sanders his Head Gardener, Gee the Head Gamekeeper, Mrs Vince in charge of the Chalet, Budd the Head Coachman and so the list continues.

Security

There were some unusual additions to the general picture of staff at Halton. Alfred had certain foibles, a nervous disposition being one. Thus, although many of the furnishings of the main house were hidden under covers for most of the year, in his absence he still arranged for his estate employees to be

formed into a part-time, personal fire brigade of eleven firemen, together with their fire engine with its Shand-Mason steam pumps and ladders - the most up to date of their kind at the turn of the century.

Their chief was Jack Hubbard, the son of the Agent of the estates. In the photograph above he has a shoulder lanyard, with a chain across his chest and stands on the extreme left of his team, almost at right angles to them. Beside him stands his deputy and chief assistant, Mr Dade, second from the left. After these in order left to right are - Mr George Budd, whose skills with horses in his work as Head Coachman must have been invaluable, Tom White, Tom Ginger, Mr Holt, Arthur Allen, Mr Norwood, Harry Spurling and Frederick Day.

Their driver, Mr Alfred White, the engineer, sits above on the engine pulled by horses - a mixture of ancient and modern power. The engine and horses were kept in the stable yard of the Grange - the Agent's House - to which the ringing of a large bell, wafting over the estate, summoned them when there was a fire.

Halton House was thus well equipped to deal with fire. Internally each floor and corridor was provided with several, usually at least six, monogrammed fire buckets, fire-extinguisher bottle bombs and Merryweather firepumps.

Indeed, security was also a high priority. In the early years two private police officers were seconded from Buckinghamshire Constabulary. Later Alfred employed his own full-time

Wg Cdr Al Sarjeant

South view of Halton House

North view of Halton House

Billiard Room Mirror

Billiard Room Mouldings

Billiard Room laid for dinner 1986

Salon Lamp

View from Salon through Ante Room to West Wing

Salon Dome and Chandelier

The Salon

Ante Room and South Drawing Room

The Grand Staircase

The Grand Staircase

Grand Staircase
Balustrade detail

The Gold or Alhambra Room 1986

The Cascade after restoration 1996

The Cascade and Pool 1996

The Belvedere

Stewards at Halton House 1954

Salon Dome and Belvedere

A walk to the Fountain

Wg Cdr Al Sarjeant

North View from the Fountain

Watercolour of Halton House by John Hull

Sunset Ceremony, Battle of Britain Parade, September 2002

security police. One, Mr Albert Zenthon, joined Halton from the Metropolitan Police Force, where he had been Station Sergeant, another was Mr Dade, one of three brothers employed on the estate in different capacities. These, together with the latest in burglar alarm systems and iron spikes on all exterior stable and kitchen walls, ensured the safety of Alfred's holiday retreat, to such effect that when an attempt at robbery was made the burglar was caught by Mr Walker, another security guard.

Victorian household staffs were estimated to average from ten to fifty in number. Halton must have employed over seventy in the house, with over eighty outdoors as grooms, gardeners, keepers, and foresters, not including casual helpers, estate workers and the eccentric additions of members of the circus and orchestra - who were employed on a semi-regular basis.

Halton was a little world on its own, generating its own industry, whether its master were at home or not, its staff far outnumbering its owner and the guests for which it had been created.

The North Elevation

CHAPTER 8

Front Entrance

THE
MAIN HOUSE

. . . a vast expenditure having been made with regard to the furniture and appointments, in addition to a lavish outlay on the building itself. Bucks Herald

THE GROUND FLOOR

Alfred was in his 30's when he inherited Halton and in his 40's when his dream house became reality. It embodied all the latest refinements and inventions and showed off his latest acquisitions and works of art. It made an appropriately baroque and absurdly theatrical setting, which, by historical accident, has preserved in its stucco decorations, the opulence, the frivolity and the confidence of the 1880's. The main house, naturally, was where the most care was lavished.

Basement

Once built, the basement was the preserve of the servants, its windows, where they faced outward, looked only onto the sunken wall of the alleyway. It was thus hidden from the eyes of the dwellers in the main house except for one peculiar circumstance.

Alfred was noted for the way he changed his mind with decorations, colouring, lights, hangings, furniture and paintings. Between Halton and Seamore Place, his house in London, paintings and furnishings in particular, shuttled to and fro, so that it is often hard to tell where certain articles were at any one time.

In Halton, shortly after the house was finished and furnished, Alfred made a big change in the basement by sweeping away the menservants' smoking room and replacing it by a 'newfangled' swimming bath.

This room, lit by two small windows towards the top of an extremely high wall contains the white-tiled, sunken bath, about $4\frac{1}{2}$ feet below floor level at the point of entry, sloping to about 5 feet at the further end. It measures about 20 by 15 feet, contains a large plug in one corner and would have been entered by a ladder from the floor of the room, alongside. This room contained a fireplace and a blue 'Turkey' carpet covered the floor. Just beyond is a marble-floored shower room and dressing room. It appears that this plunge, or swimming bath, was for cold water only. A spiral staircase with stone steps and a graceful, wrought-iron balustrade, with mahogany handrail, winds down from the main house for access to this arctic innovation.

Ground Floor Entrance

The visitor to Halton would arrive under a porte cochere - a carriage porch of golden stone, much carved, open on all sides and sweeping into a graceful arch overhead. This leads up two steps into a smaller porch, and then by three more, wide, white steps to the great double doors. These swing open into a parquet-floored and half-panelled entrance hall.

THE VISITOR TO HALTON WOULD ARRIVE UNDER A PORTE COCHERE - A CARRIAGE PORCH OF GOLDEN STONE, MUCH CARVED, OPEN ON ALL SIDES AND SWEEPING INTO A GRACEFUL ARCH OVERHEAD.

Beyond are two more pairs of glass-panelled doors, between which survive the original, gold silk-damask wall hangings. There we meet one of the first elaborately plastered ceilings, still unaltered - one of the hallmarks of this house. The pattern is picked out with gold leaf, as bright today as the day it was made, the central part of which resembles the ceiling of the garden entrance room opposite.

The door fittings too deserve a second look - the brass knobs bear the five arrows of the Rothschilds and the finger plates carry the AR monogram of Alfred de Rothschild. Even the keyhole covers are decorated. There are also useful brass cups set opposite the door handles to prevent damage to the walls or frames. It is with little features like these that the builder illustrates his mastery over the smallest details - something frequently found in this mansion.

SALON

The entrance hall leads into the salon, the largest room in the house. In some plans it is called the salon and in others the central hall. Despite its size, its function was for reading, meeting and socialising. It rises up through two central floors of the house - over 31 feet high, to a magnificent glass dome overhead. From pillar to pillar the salon is about 48 feet long by 30 feet wide. It extends beyond the pillars - on one side to the anteroom between the drawing rooms, and on the other to the grand staircase. Among the Rothschild houses the salon compares only with that in the earlier Mentmore Towers, which also had a glass roof and a first floor gallery overlooking the room. The effect at Halton is made lighter by the introduction of large mirrors, together with many high arches, at ground and

GROUND FLOOR PLAN OF MAIN HOUSE

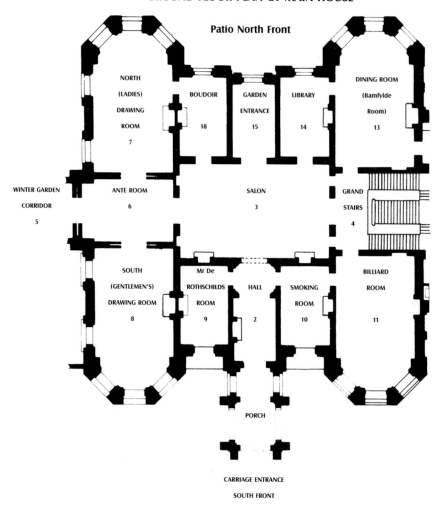

68

Salon 1887

first floor level, under the ceiling and with the familiar five Rothschild arrows.

One album of photographs, preserved in the Officers' Mess, is signed and dated 1888. Further pictures, however, range over about a twenty-year period. The earliest of these were probably taken by Thompson of Grosvenor Square, who had already taken photographs of some of Alfred's antiques for publication in 1884.

Other interiors were taken by Mr Henry Bedford Lemere, a famous London architectural photographer, whose offices in The Strand were opposite the Gaiety Theatre. His earliest work dates from before 1884, and his large glass negatives, all 12" x 10", have turned his prints into collectors' pieces, since they show every detail so clearly. He records that he was working at Halton in 1892, so many of the later photographs must be his work.

The earliest photographs show the salon as it probably was in 1887, filled with heavily buttoned, fringed, velvet and leather chairs, a few small Louis XVI tables, ornate candelabras, gilt and ormolu Benares peacocks used for Pot Pourri, pots for flowers, some matching commodes, white marble statues in the four corners and curtains, to keep out draughts, looped back within the arches upstairs and down. These curtains were of chinese silk, embroidered with gold thread and lined with blue silk or flowered Utrecht velvet. On the floor is an enormous Persian carpet and above is a huge waterfall of a crystal chandelier, resplendent with candles and suspended from the dome. Contemporary accounts tell us that the wall panels of silk damask specially commissioned from Spitalfields, were crimson and the plasterwork white, so the room must have had an almost overpowering effect.

A close-up of the centre of the room just catches the dainty cabriole leg of one of a pair of Leleu tables, and highlights the piece that dominates the room, a big circular conversation sofa (complete with footstools) from the middle of which springs a miniature garden of flowers and ferns. Behind these is the arch to the main entrance doors.

Close-up of Salon 1887

Salon 1892

Hanging on the walls on either side, above the bronze and ormolu candelabra supported by draped female figures, are two oval paintings by the French artist Boucher, of about 1743. On the left of the door is "Cupid disarmed by Venus", where the goddess with two white doves at her feet holds up Cupid's quiver, which he is trying to reach. On the right is "Venus caressing Cupid". The gold frames are ornate, surmounted by a quiver, a flaming torch and two birds touching beaks, similar to the pairs of birds decorating the present bases of the pillars. On the opposite side of the salon were two further paintings by Boucher, completed after 1750, "The Toilet of Venus" and the "Birth and Triumph of Venus".

Another group of photographs show the same room taken about 1892. The most obvious change is the chandelier. It is now a full blown electrolier. Gone are the lustres. The fifty-one electric fittings are enclosed by tulip-shaped, upright bowls on an ornate gilt metal frame decorated with acanthus leaves. The frame closely resembles the one in place today.

Below the furniture has changed. Gone are the heavy armchairs and the buttons!

In their place are smaller and more comfortable padded chairs, gay with cut velvet and beauvais tapestry in greens and reds. The backs illustrated variously the arts, the sciences, the seasons, children and animals; the seats displayed industrial occupations, birds, animals and children. Delicate dining chairs invite guests to sit at one or other of the pair of fine Louis XVI writing desks to examine the collection of small art objects on them. Others might be tempted to glance at the occasional tables set with writing paper and a visitors' book or to search on the lower shelves for the latest poems and novels fresh from the presses. The bowls of plants of earlier years have grown and flourished, as have the central decorations of the sofa. Shades have appeared on lamps and candelabra, and a new pair of magnificent French tables with Italian marble tops take the place of the commodes. The effect is lighter and brighter.

The biggest change, however, we can see today. No doubt the earlier red silk wall panels had been chosen to show off Alfred's paintings. Here, the panels and paintings have vanished, to be replaced by plaster-work of musical instruments,

Crown Copyright 2003

The Grand Staircase

(Left) Plaster panel of musical instruments.

The Grand Staircase sweeps into the salon in wide stately steps beyond the pillars - surely a very early example of open planning. It rises to a half-landing and then divides and continues upwards on either side of the stairwell, until it meets the main landing and gallery. This part of the gallery resembles a bridge dividing the stairwell from the salon.

The staircase walls were panelled and fitted to take large paintings or tapestries. Another large, but this time rectangular, curved glass ceiling reminiscent of Paxton's Crystal Palace - lights the stairs and suspends above it another fine crystal chandelier - this one can be winched up and down for replacement of lights, unlike that in the salon.

The present chandelier came from the central dome of the winter garden and was removed before the building was demolished. "Myself (Mr Coe) and Mr Laker, electricians for AMWD, took a fortnight to dismantle, mark and label the chandelier in 1936 and we placed it over the main stairs a year later. There was no winch or power coming from the centre of the glass ceiling over the stair at that time, so we had to install these. The original wiring was in place but disconnected". While this work was being done the crystal spires, drops, tulip-shades and fittings, packed in boxes and weighing half-a-ton, were stored in the basement battery room. "Unfortunately, half the glass went missing" . . . and

moulded in relief, so that the salon begins to resemble the room with which we are now familiar.

It must have been at this time also, or very shortly afterwards, that the raised plasterwork on walls and ceilings was heavily encrusted with gold leaf. Indeed, there is a veritable epidemic of plasterwork everywhere. It outlines the pillars and edges the panels. It wreathes the mirrors and adds decorative musical instruments, leaves, shells, cherubs, birds or symbols of the hunt in accessible and inaccessible places. It forms rounders of fish and fowl above doors and on ceilings, or represents Alfred's initials and the famous five arrows (occasionally varied with three).

Stucco decoration is quicker as well as daintier than the carved woodwork found in such houses as Waddesdon, where Ferdinand had transported whole rooms from demolished Paris properties. Thus at Halton in the main house, plasterwork encrusts most walls and ceilings of the ground floor and gallery but diminishes in the bedrooms, until it finally disappears altogether on other floors, clearly marking the division between the public and private areas of the mansion.

Taken in 1887, with plain finial, statue on half-landing and plain panels.

Top landing of grand staircase. Reversed arrows and AR monogram panels can be clearly seen. Beyond are the three balcony arches.

although there had originally been five tiers to the chandelier "with lots gone, I'm sorry to say, it went back as best we could". Finally the chandelier was reformed, with difficulty, into two tiers.

In Alfred's time the stairbase on the ground floor was lined with palms and flowers and eventually there were bronze cupids holding aloft further candelabra at the stairfoot. The wrought-iron scroll balustrade, in black and gold,

Stairfoot looking through arches to the salon.

was produced in London with Alfred's monogram and the family arrows set alternately along its length. The arrows unfortunately were set the wrong way, with points up instead of down, but there must have been too little time for them to be changed - so there they remain to this day. The handrail itself is in highly polished brass.

The ceiling frescoes around the skylight are heavily patterned with heads and leaves in gold leaf, but at the foot of the staircase and under it, ceilings become simpler, although one design incorporates the familiar Rothschild arrows. The stairfoot of polished wooden tiles was covered with priceless Persian carpets and furnished with small Louis XV consoles, side tables and chairs. In addition, it was here that Alfred elected to place his Orchestrion, made by Imhof and Muckle, by the aid of whose 41 cylinders he was able to entertain himself or his guests with a wide virtuoso performance. The prize of Alfred's collection, however, stood with their backs to the pillars, facing the staircase - a magnificent pair of tall Chinese vases while looking down on them, from the half landing, was a fine white marble statue, (changed from time to time by Alfred) surrounded with flowers and ferns.

Alfred hung a huge Beauvais tapestry by Neilson on the wall above the half-landing. It features an eastern scene, shaded by a very chinese looking pavilion. The plasterwork flanking this was obviously made with the tapestry in mind, since at the top of the two side panels a canopy imitating the pavilion is introduced. This feature appears four times on the side walls of the downstairs staircase corridors, but nowhere else.

The Winter Garden

Balancing the kitchen wing at the opposite end of the mansion was the octagonal winter garden. Many Victorians boasted conservatories in their houses - advances in glass and iron techniques encouraged them to be more spectacular in design - but few built to the size and elaboration of Alfred de Rothschild. Using the basement for its water tanks and heating, and built on a raised ground floor platform, the winter garden could be viewed from inside the house through sliding, plate-glass doors beyond the drawing rooms or from a little tea table set amidst the mosaics, plants and statues of the entrance corridor. It was large enough to contain a Hungarian Orchestra, a Circus, a central statue of a Dancing Girl by Canova or an instant garden. Upholstered sofas, little tables and Persian carpets allowed a

Winter Garden

guest to sit on its fringe and admire the flowers, the palms and the marbles or to enjoy the wild delights of nature in civilised comfort. Much play was made of varying levels both inside and out, so that you went down steps into it, and up and down steps out of it.

It was almost all glass and plaster, being dominated by a massive central glass dome topped by a secondary dome above. Eight small domes were ranged around it and there was an extra roof-light over the entrance passage leading from the house. The temperature was always kept at a steady 63 degrees fahrenheit summer and winter, and

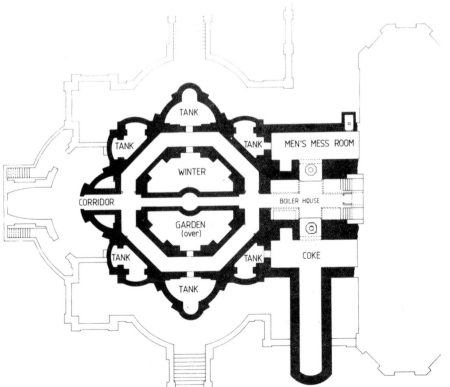

Winter Garden basement

Interior of the Winter Garden

Alfred was most particular about the flowers and arrangements inside.

There is a story that at one time he wanted climbing roses in bloom to cover some of the supporting pillars. The gardener could not get immediate results, so after a climbing rose had been uprooted, transferred and then induced to drape its foliage artistically against the whiteness of the pillar, some substitute foliage was added with artificial roses to give more height and colour. When Alfred returned some time later he did not comment on this unnatural speed, instead he merely glanced, nodded and was satisfied. The overall result was enough.

A kind of passageway, surrounded by seven, three-windowed bays, ran around the central garden core. Visitors could then open the windows and step outside onto a pretty balcony from which descended three shallow flights of steps to the outside gardens. Truly, Alfred's winter garden was a most impressive sight.

*Passageway with seven
three-windowed bays
running around the
central Winter Garden
core*

It survived into the 1930's when eventually it was replaced by a square building containing Royal Air Force single officers' accommodation.

Ante Room

Between the winter garden and the salon runs a corridor. But this is no ordinary passageway. Between the drawing rooms, it widens and forms a square ante-room. Its four, ceiling-high arches, one in each wall, are capable of being entirely closed off by plaster-decorated and painted doors, matching those in the salon. It can thus become a room in its own right or an extension of either the salon or the drawing rooms, which lie on either side of it. Sometimes it was used to house an orchestra to entertain guests. An interesting feature of the west arch of this ante-chamber is that it presented its owner with four options. It could be left open as a corridor, closed with green curtains, become a sliding door decorated in gold as all the other doors were, or be transformed by doors inset with enormous panes of what must have been extremely heavy and good quality glass. These not only gave the ante room enough light but visitors could view the delights of the winter garden through the glass. The doors, which fitted flush into the wall recesses,

were grasped by neat flat handles, raised by a fingertip. They slide across today as easily as when they were made.

The gold-decorated ceiling incorporates four rounders in relief - no details picked out in colour - of clouds, little cherubs and temples. Above the doors to each drawing room is the now familiar AR monogram. This was the simplest and least cluttered room of the house, because of its function as a corridor.

Ante Room

North drawing room looking towards bay windows, with fireplace and door, now gone, on the right

furnishings and, of course, in art works. Each has a large bay of three arched windows, with two more along one wall. These are fitted with wooden shutters and decorated to match the rest of the room. At the entrance of each room a four-part door fills the high arch, into which each smaller part can be slid back individually. When Alfred was entertaining a large house party, where greater space was required, the opened arches could turn the two drawing rooms, with the ante-room between, into one long reception chamber.

The North or Ladies' Drawing Room

The north drawing room, as with all four corner rooms on this floor, is about 45$\frac{1}{2}$ feet long, 26 feet wide, and nearly 17 feet high. The main ceiling contains a cream coloured oval set in an oblong, the space between crisscrossed with gold lattice work, like icing on a wedding cake. It looks delicate and fits the purpose of the room. In the patternwork of the coving can again be seen Alfred's initials, only in the two drawing rooms they can be read as ACR, Alfred Charles de Rothschild.

Charming vignettes of an eighteenth century lady and gentleman courting, playing music or dancing, decorate the four corners of the main ceiling, while a lively scene of cupids divides the ceiling of the bay from the rest of the room. Only

The walls were lined with silk - the decorative battens are still visible - and hung with four matching paintings, at one time by Boucher and later of flowers and fruit by Van Huysum, (now in the Getty Museum, USA). Lining the sides were Louis XVI sofas, upholstered in red, while in the middle was an imposing, heavy, carved, Victorian table with a marble top.

DRAWING ROOMS

The two drawing rooms stand opposite one another, separated by the antechamber. They are a mirror image of each other in decor, but differ slightly in

North drawing room

*North Drawing Room
1892*

one chandelier lit the room as Alfred had several wall and table lights, but today three carefully copied chandeliers take its place.

The room also contains a white and dark red marble fireplace, similar to the one in the other room, topped with a huge arched mirror, though the mirror has disappeared, in the same way as the small doorway between this room and the ladies' boudoir next door.

In Alfred's day, this gold and white room was filled with furniture, much of it Louis XV period - chairs, tables, sofas and cabinets, down to the delicate Savonnerie carpet made in France and the clock in the bay and on the mantlepiece. The trolleys are covered in velvets and in the middle of the room stands the obligatory round sofa with its central flower decoration. Its upholstery, however, is sprigged with flowers and has a draped and fringed base matching the fringe on some of the Victorian easy chairs scattered around. Surprisingly, neither they, nor the other chairs and sofas, have the matching all-over patterns of the salon.

In the 1892 photograph, Alfred shows off two huge white marble urns in the window overlooking the side terrace, with a corner of the winter garden in the background. Between these, against the wall, is a magnificent cabinet containing plaques inlaid with semi-precious marbles, while on the wall above is "The Toilet of Venus" by Veronese, flanked on either side by a flower painting by Van Huysum, dating from about 1722. On the further wall is a glimpse of one of the early Italian paintings in Alfred's collection, the Magdalen, wearing a blue gown over a red dress, and painted by Domenichino. The opened arch at the end of the room looks across the anteroom to the south drawing room opposite.

The French windows of this room all opened onto a wide balconied terrace, where guests could walk, admire and take the air.

Later in his life, as Alfred's art collection grew, the contents of this room again changed. Reynolds painting of Lady Bamfylde moved from the dining room and replaced the Gainsborough. Opposite, as a companion piece, was Reynolds painting from 1784-7, of Mary Elizabeth Duchess of Rutland, in a black dress and white scarf. This had hung opposite Lady Bamfylde in the dining room after its purchase in 1894, until Alfred decided to bring them both into what was essentially a ladies' withdrawing room. To these he added

*Detail of ceiling, North
Drawing Room*

another Lady Hamilton in morning dress by Romney, and two Cuyps of landscapes with rivers and figures.

South Drawing Room

This drawing room was primarily for gentlemen, containing as it did Alfred's grand piano, modestly hidden under draperies, and some of his most prized paintings. There is still a profusion of armchairs and side tables, but fewer straight-backed dining chairs and few chairs without arms. It faced the front of the Mansion and over-looked the arriving carriages and guests.

Among the noteworthy furnishings are a pair of Sèvres vases and a clock in a vase-shaped case on the mantel, a pair of silver statues on the brackets on either side of the fireplace - one being a sixteenth century work of Diana seated on a stag and set with pearls, rubles and diamonds, the other being St George and the Dragon. The room also contained a number of other pieces of Sèvres china, vases, jardinieres for holding plants, some little Sèvres tables and a pair of Louis XVI cabinets.

The paintings were mostly smaller works, but by outstanding artists. Near the window were two small portraits by Rembrandt, of a man and a woman, together with two works by Watteau and two by Pater, a painter who worked in the romantic style of Watteau. There was a fine picture of Lady Templeton by the English artist Thomas Lawrence, after whom Alfred named the room, but with his usual unpredictability, Alfred later removed this work, although the room continued to be called the Lawrence room. On the right of the arch to the ante-room, hung the painting of Mademoiselle Duthe by Drouais.

Alfred seems to have liked this room, since he chose to have his photograph taken in a corner near the bay window overlooking the balcony and front porch. Here he sits at ease, in his Louis XV armchair, under his favourite painting of "Les Amants Heureux" - The Happy Lovers by Pater. He is master of all he surveys and looks a picture of pride and content. As this photograph appears in all the earliest albums of before 1888, Alfred must have been in his early forties at the time. This portrait was therefore, roughly contemporary with the earliest period of the house.

Alfred de Rothschild in the corner of the South drawing room.

South Drawing Room looking towards the arch where the doors have been slid out of sight.

No doubt it was to this room that Alfred brought his guests to sing or play his piano and to entertain or be entertained, when he had only a small houseparty. But if it were a larger occasion with extra visitors, then the two drawing rooms would be thrown open, or even the salon would be pressed into service, and the liquid notes of a guest singer would float out, or the violin of Elman would throb in the evening stillness. There were few occasions, when Alfred entertained, that music was not present in its most spellbinding form.

By 1918, paintings in this room included Dutch landscapes by:

Wouverman	- a landscape, horsemen and figures
Wouverman	- a hawking party
Wouverman	- a shooting party
Wouverman	- a landscape, horsemen and figures
Van der Velde	- Cattle with Shepherd and Shepherdess
Paul Potter	- Cattle and homestead
Pynaker	- Landscape, cattle and figures
Berghem	- Landscape, cattle and figures

Also included were two dainty, pre-revolutionary French works, which acted

South Drawing Room from the Ante Room.

as companions to the other Watteaus and Paters. These were: Lancret - Garden scene with fountain and figures, and Netscher - Lady in a satin dress seated at a table. These small genre works had survived Alfred's large scale sale of many small French works, prior to his death.

The small cabinet to the left of the fireplace also displayed a large number of very fine miniatures by a selection of artists, such as Cosway, Boucher, Hilliard and Holbein.

Mr De Rothchild's Room

Alfred must have favoured the colour red. The salon was red, his dressing room was known as the red dressing room, and there were 'Red' rooms in his London House. This room, the one private to him when he resided here, his business room, was also called the Red Room. It is true that it was a small room in comparison with others in this part of the house; it was only 15 feet wide by 25 feet long, and led straight out of the entrance hall. The decoration of the

ceiling was more restrained and so is the general appearance - Roth attributes the elaboration of detail elsewhere to Rogers but the greater simplicity here to Alfred's own taste. That can be challenged as the room and furnishings are still far from simple! The veined black and grey marble fireplace and the chandelier give a different impression, while the furnishings are very valuable - each a collector's piece. However, there is less furniture and there are fewer paintings - which may be accounted 'simplicity'.

Alfred's Louis XIV bureau Mazarin, or brass, leather and gilt writing-desk, faces another of his earliest favourite art works - the portrait of Lady Hamilton by Romney. The cabinet by Cresson carries a Louis XVI ormolu and white marble clock and candelabra, while the bookcase facing us, has a central Louis XVI ormolu clock by Lepine and also a pair of terra cotta busts of Baccantes by Marin. There are three Sèvres vases in pale blue together with candelabra on the mantlepiece, while leaves fill the fireplace. Of the other paintings, one on the left of the bookcase is the "Musical

Mr de Rothschilds room

Smoking room, 1892

Peasants" by Berghem painted in about 1645. The remainder are mainly landscapes and seascapes. Flowers, seals, little pieces made at Sèvres or by Faberge, a finely-tooled leather diary, a cigar case and ashtray, books and an empire inkstand are placed deliberately on the desk, both as decoration and for use, showing Alfred's personal choice in small objects.

Later he brought Romney's picture of Lady Paulett to Halton and hung it as a pair with Lady Hamilton. The heads of Bacchantes gave way to portrait busts of two of Alfred's favourite Frenchmen, Voltaire and Rousseau, while the third of his favourites, Cardinal Richelieu, painted by Phillipe de Champaigne, gazed down on him from the wall. In this room he also hung one work, out of the thirteen he owned, by the Flemish painter Teniers. This, the largest and actually the one he liked best, was called "A Village Festival". He also found space to include a bust and painting of an eighteenth century man.

No doubt the ubiquitous telephone lurked also in some dark corner for the Master of the house to keep in touch with friends and business left behind in London, or to give his instructions to valet, agent, housekeeper or butler on his present visit to his mansion.

The Smoking Room

On the opposite side of the entrance hall opens another room, possibly the finest and certainly the most interesting in the mansion. This was intended as the gentlemen's sanctum, the place where men could smoke undisturbed by the company of the ladies, who disapproved of such pollution. Houses of this period frequently contained Moorish, Alhambra or Indian rooms - following the questionable fashion of the dear Queen - and Alfred made his smoking room into his Arab room. Its beauty is in its magnificent ceiling, patterned into circles and all kinds of geometrical shapes in burnished gold leaf, down to its brass rails and alcoves. Its cost was reputed to be in the region of £25,000 in Alfred's day. Arches and gold hangings line the walls, a pair of fine brass-panelled, folding doors open into the room, and the hanging light and fireplace strive to contribute a suitably Moorish touch

A pair of full size, gilt Eastern figures on plinths, decorate the corners, while practically everything else - chairs, table, couch, piano, even the palm that so dominates the scene - is distinctly Victorian. Adding to this medley are a French antique clock and candelabra.

When Alfred grew older his taste matured and his collection extended. As a consequence this room changed its appearance. The alterations began with his purchases of Italian and Spanish Old Master works, and his conscious decision to concentrate them into two rooms at Seamore Place and one at Halton. The fine "Portrait of a Young Nobleman" by Bronzino, turned this gold room into a "Bronzino" room. He then added the Spanish "St Joseph and the Infant Christ"

by Murillo, the Flemish "Figures in a Landscape" by Rembrandt and two other early Italian portraits of gentlemen. Also, mounted on the walls in velvet, were displayed a small selection of circular shields, some in silver and one of steel damascened in gold and silver by the master craftsman Negroli. To give a suitable setting to these and miscellaneous other pieces of armour, including two pairs of Boutet pistols, he changed the wall coverings to green silk damask, the curtains to green velvet and tinsel, and replaced the hanging light with lustres.

How many times have guests in this room regaled one another on their mistakes or triumphs in the billiard room next door, or come to recover from an exciting game in a haze of cigar smoke and conversation?

The Billiard Room

This room matched the other three big corner rooms in size and is about 26 feet

The Billiard Room. The damask panel on the far wall was later replaced by a large mirror.

wide by 42½ feet long. Large though it seems, its function was purely for playing billiards. The game, after being in existence for several centuries, had reached a peak of popularity. The difficulty in most houses was finding a room light enough and large enough to house a full-sized table. In a place like Halton, a room could be designed specifically for the purpose.

Accordingly, the room was dominated by an extremely fine table, its exposed woodwork carved and gilded to match the decoration of the room. The marigold, so often found in other places and rooms, is prominent in the design perhaps it was a favourite of Alfred or his decorator.

To match the table, the main parts of the walls are veneered in wood, and the doors are also left in their natural state, except for the gilt edging on their panels and the semi-circular mouldings of the muses of music and the symbols of Apollo above them. Half-relief pillars with heavy gold capitals uphold plaster coving, painted to imitate wood. In keeping with this style, the ceiling is painted to resemble heavy wooden beams, its ridges moulded and gilded with white panels deep-set between, patterned with family arrows, Alfred's monogram, laurel wreaths and other designs. The plaster work on the walls also depicts symbols of arts and sciences while the lower panels carry Alfred's monogram in a rather more obvious and flamboyant form than usual.

The room changed its appearance even in Alfred's time. In earlier photographs the table was lit by a number of small overhead lamps. In later photographs this was replaced by larger fittings. In the same way the damask-hung walls of the earliest days gave way to more woodwork and an extra mirror facing the windows - to give more light in an essentially dark brown room. The additional wood panels were decorated with gilt plaster motifs at the top, as in the salon where the panels were probably altered at about the same time.

The white marble fireplace was the second of the two dominating features in this room. It displays two large female figures carved in relief, in the manner of the Greek Caryatids, one holding a ridded urn and the other a laurel wreath. Between them is inset a small, Italian, carved plaque of classical figures. On the mantel above, reflected in the arched mirror, are a pair of dark-coloured urns, a pair of Chinese vases in famille rose and a fine matching jardiniere containing a plant.

The table was islanded by a Persian carpet square, outside which assorted chairs and sofas for spectators lined the walls. Indeed, there was a platform under the central chesterfield to enable those sitting in this position to have a better view. Above is a painting of a man by Jordaens, later replaced by the "Duchess of Richmond in Satin with Cupids" by Van Dyke paired with a portrait of Madame Elizabeth (sister of Louis XVI) by Raoux. After some years this was changed to a landscape by Wynants, lit from the side by fine, bowl-like Chinese celadon lamps. Nearby were billiard cues, while a side table set with a decorative lamp, shared another wall with an elaborately framed gold and brown score board. Nearby, for those who tired of the game, was a glass case displaying small objects in Chinese jade and porcelain. There were also two large baize-lined fitted cupboards for equipment storage.

The Gun Room

Though near the billiard room, this retreat properly lay in the servants' wing, indicating clearly those who were chiefly concerned with the daily care of its contents. It was isolated by doors from the remainder of the house and accessible from the secondary staircase, the luggage entrance and the gentlemen's toilets. In similar houses this room often formed a bridge between staff and family, where both sides of the household met to plan or criticise shoots, to maintain the weapons and to chat generally.

Alfred did not enjoy this sport but he took part in it, as was expected of him. However, it may be suspected that his main interest lay in the quality of the guns themselves. He obviously valued his set of Purdey guns and Boutet pistols.

His pleasure chiefly lay in seeing the enjoyment of those who used them - perhaps even in the welfare of the animals involved. Here, in row upon shining row, would lodge the weapons that cost a fortune, well-oiled, polished and ready for use in their locked cupboards. Women perhaps ventured into the billiard room - several of the ladies among Alfred's house guests were noted players - but none would dare to enter this territory.

THE DINING ROOM

Facing the billiard room on the other side of the grand staircase is the dining room. Though resembling the room it once was, it has seen many changes in structure and function. In Alfred's day it was decorated in gold and white and much admired for its large painting of Lady Bamfylde by Sir Joshua Reynolds. Indeed, several of Alfred's friends so liked the picture that he commissioned copies, a particularly fine one going to his friend, Lord Kitchener. The room, therefore, was known as the Bamfylde Room and the work was specifically left to the National Gallery after his death.

The painting shows a dark-eyed rather sharpfaced beauty with expressive hands, wearing a loose dress and draperies, her hair in the tall wig and shoulder-dangling ringlet of the eighteenth century. She leans nonchalantly on a wall, spread with a lily-painted cloth, in the shade of a tree. Behind her is a sweeping landscape, typical of Reynolds at his best.

Dining Room Fireplace 1887.

Beside the lady, the splendours of the rest of the room recede into insignificance, the set of Beauvais tapestry panels by Neilson dating from 1764, the matching set of Louis XV gilt and tapestried chairs, the commodes, the tapestry firescreen, the mosaic tables, the oval Louis XVI table made by De Louisville and the finest Chinese celadon bowls and bases. In fact, the little dining table set for one with pristine white napery looks almost lost on the wide expanse of Turkish carpet.

This room boasts another fine marble fireplace, but not so large as that in the billiard room where the fireplace had to compete in scale with the large table. This fireplace is daintier. The relief-carved ladies stand on pedestals and carry the appropriate flowers and wine, while across the lintel dancing classical females accompany the carriage of Venus, between large baskets of fruit and flowers. The classical theme is followed in the standing figures supporting the candelabra and clock, and is continued into the crossed, ivyleaved thyrsus of Bacchus, god of wine, which decorates some of the ceiling panels together with the lyre of Apollo, god of music. The four rounders in the corners of the ceiling depict river and sea food and game, while over the entrance door to the room, flanking the Rothschild arrows, are two cornucopia spilling out of their horns an abundance of fruits and flowers of the season. Of incidental interest is the fact that of the two original doors on the salon side of the room, one is merely part of the matching decoration and opens only to a shallow cupboard.

Beyond this room was the servery where the Butler heated up dishes and marshalled his footmen. This area has seen much change, however, and the addition of another corridor leading to a new and much larger dining room, makes it more suited to the needs of the greater number of present-day occupants.

The old dining room, however, could hold many more diners than the one of the picture above. On more festive occasions fifty or more could be accommodated. A later photograph (shown on page 52) shows Trodd the

Dining for one, 1887.

Butler with twin footmen in attendance, presiding over a room crowded with small, spindly, gilt chairs and round tables, all beautifully decorated with serviettes, fruit and flowers from Alfred's own hothouses.

This picture, more than any other, perhaps better captures the spirit of the room when the house was fulfilling its role of entertaining Alfred's guests. From 1907, paintings to be found here were four works by Cuyp "The Watering Place", "Castle with some Peasants", a "Self-Portrait" and "Flight Into Egypt". Lady Bamfylde by this time has been moved elsewhere. The room also later contained several Beauvais tapestries.

The Library

This was a room for an art lover not a student. In fact, apart from a more elaborate ceiling, it could easily be mistaken for the Red Room, Alfred's own room, which it much resembles, except that the colour here is gold, as can be seen from the gold silk damask still around the walls.

The low bookcase and neatly tooled, stacked books are almost an afterthought - part of the decoration! Here Alfred could contemplate not only small paintings of the Dutch School, but also an unusual cabinet with curved sides containing smaller objects - collector's pieces such as rock crystal bases, silver gilt cups, tankards and ornate salt cellars.

Above the door is a landscape by Ruysdael and above the Cabinet is an

Library.

Library looking into the salon.

interior view of a picture gallery by Tenieres, while landscapes and towns-folk of the seventeenth century line the walls, two deep in most cases. On the right of the cabinet is a "Village Wedding" by Jan Steen, and below it "The Fruit Stall" by Van Ostade, while on the other side are two "Landscapes with Hawking Parties" by Wouverman and other landscapes by Berghem, with "A

Scene of Gentlemen Drinking" by De Hooch nearby. Paintings by artists of the same school hang on other walls.

A fine French writing table in ormolu by Martin Carlin, stands in the centre of the room, which is comfortably furnished with easy chairs, as well as a set of matching regency gilt dining chairs, all finished in rich cut velour. The fireplace follows the prevailing style, its white marble being decorated with gilded brass. Two small round tables with Sèvres tops stand on either side of the fireplace, matching the two jardinieres with plant bulbs on the table and the fine Sèvres pieces above the fireplace.

Later, when Alfred came to change things round, the paintings in this room altered almost completely with the sole exception of Teniers' "Picture Gallery". Alfred had by now reluctantly allowed his collection to include some Rubens.

"Such a pity" commented a friend, "but then, they are famous!" Mrs Lionel de Rothschild considered, however, that Alfred had very few favourites among his paintings - unless they were all his favourites. "He never showed a preference for any school of painting or any period of art". The changes, chiefly of Dutch Paintings of a similar period show methodical arrangement, but it is noticeable that no works from this room were willed to anyone!

Later paintings to be found in this room included:

Rubens	- Figure subjects
Rubens	- Rape of the Sabines
Terborche	- The Guitar Lesson
Mieris	- A Musical Evening
Netscher	- Lady in a Cream and Blue Satin Dress
Wynants	- Interior of Artists Studio with Artists at Work
Wynants	- Landscape with Figures and Hawks
Wouverman	- Camp Scene with Horseman
Teniers	- Exterior with Figures
J Ostade	- Exterior with Figures
A Ostade	- Villagers Dancing
Backhuysen	- Coast Scene with Fishing Boats and Figures
J Jones	- (a print from Romney) Emma Hamilton
Van der Heyden	- Exterior, Buildings and Figures

THE GARDEN ENTRANCE

During Alfred's day this room stood opposite the south entrance and its French window led straight onto the paved terrace outside. From here guests could see the famous three-spray fountain and the rose bushes along the "ravelled walk up to the fountain's edge." As with all the rooms it was richly furnished with a chandelier, an ornate marble-topped gilt table, a pier glass reflecting yet more Sèvres vases and jardinieres containing plants, some cabinets, chairs and sofas, and a round central table - heavily draped - used for depositing hats and gloves, as this was not so much a room as a passageway from the salon to the north garden. The glass-panelled doors, usually pushed back into recesses in the walls, lent light to the salon, but heavy curtains kept back

the draughts. The ceiling, supported by two pairs of pillars in relief, in keeping with the pillars surrounding the salon was surprisingly ornate and featured musical instruments among the decorations. At first Alfred decided to hang four paintings by Boucher on the damask-covered walls. Then, for a few years they were left unadorned.

Because of its function, this is the only room of the main suite that does not contain a fireplace.

Garden entrance looking into Salon with ornate table cover, paintings and chandelier with candles. 1887.

Garden entrance with hats on table, no paintings and tulip-shaped light fittings, 1892

Corner of the boudoir with a large painting by Gainsborough.

The Boudoir or Morning Room

Alterations during the tenure of the Royal Air Force have considerably changed this beautiful little room, meant to be used only by lady guests. Though the same fireplace remains, its white marble insets have been replaced by Royal Air Force symbols, and the wall separating it from the garden entrance has been opened up, being replaced by an arch. A glance upwards shows that the present room contains two ceilings, in which the pattern here differs markedly from that of the garden entrance alongside, being coved with a triple band of filigree ornamentation of lovers knots, medallions and flowers, broken at intervals by double upright bars.

This room was as much the preserve of the ladies as the smoking room was that of the men, its main colours being turquoise and pink, in addition to the white and gold decor of the ceiling and the gold damask walls. Alfred must have enjoyed decorating this room as it contained some of his most attractive paintings and furnishings.

In one corner is a Vernis Martin screen. The central table is elegantly draped with French tapestry and displays five gold-tooled volumes with Alfred's monogram on the front, together with a pink Chelsea china inkstand. Around the room are a few smaller Victorian armchairs, two Louis XVI sofas and a number of Louis XVI chairs with matching tapestry backs and seats. The rest of the furniture consists of little Sèvres side-tables and a magnificent small upright cabinet inlaid with large ormolu plaques made by Weisweiller, probably for Queen Marie Antoinette - possibly the most important item in Alfred's collection. A notable Louis XV clock showing a lion with its foot on a golden ball stands on one table, while Chelsea and Sèvres vases in turquoise or blue decorate most shelves, or as jardinieres, hold plants and flowers.

Like most of the others in the main house, this room had parquet flooring inlaid with a wide border of different coloured woods and patterns. Today's fitted carpets hide the craftsmanship that the Persian or Aubusson fringed rugs would have shown. The antique marble and metal fireplace here, supposed to have come from the village in the gardens of Versailles created for Queen Marie Antoinette, also shows what elsewhere is similarly hidden - a marble hearth with a decorative inlay, sometimes so deeply incised with Alfred's monogram that you can outline it with your finger. As with many of the other rooms, the dado near the floor is lined with patterned panels in white and gold. The door panels, finger plates and handles are also given a distinctive pattern. The light fitting is similar to those in most of the other rooms. The upper part is hidden by a huge gold tassel, the lower lights curve up like petals from a flower ending with the tulip-shaped, upright, glass bowls found elsewhere. In the centre beneath is a single gilded pendant.

In the early days this room was surprisingly devoid of art work. In fact, photographs of this period show only two paintings, one being a small genre French work. The other was a large impressive portrait, facing the fireplace on the wall which has now been removed. This is a bravura work, the first large scale painting by Gainsborough at his Bath studio in 1760.

It shows Ann Ford, a talented amateur musician. She holds a guitar, leans on sheets of music and there is a viola in the background. Later she became Mrs Philip Thicknesse. The unusual half-turned pose stretched Gainsborough's talents, but he is really in his element in showing the folds, the trimmings, the embroidery and the lace of the wonderful white dress she is wearing. It is a perfect foil for the colour and purpose of this room.

Something in the painting, however, displeased Alfred, so in 1894 it was sold in exchange for Reynold's "Miss Angelo", to which he added "Mrs Ticknell" by Romney to hang as a pair with "Miss Angelo", and another version of the "Duchess of Gloucester". He later, mischievously, willed the coquettish "Miss Angelo" to Mrs Leopold de Rothschild because he knew that she disapproved of it. By now the room also contained several other paintings including such smaller works as two by Greuze, one being a "Polish Lady with a Fur", together with "A Girl with Pigeons, Crossing a Stream" by Boucher, two painters much admired by Alfred and eminently suitable for a ladies' room.

Eventually the room contained at least one more Reynolds and Boucher and was filled with other paintings many of which had come from elsewhere at Halton or Seamore Place, among which were:

Drouais	- Mlle Duthe, a French courtesan (moved from the south drawing room)
Lancret	- A Garden Scene with Figures
Lancret	- A Skating Party
Lancret	- A River View with Figures
Lancret	- A French Garden Scene - Fruit Gathering
Pater	- 4 Landscapes with Figures
Cuyp	- A Dutch Skating Scene
Teniers	- Village Peasants Dancing
Jan Steen	- Dutch Street with Figures
Wouverman	- Landscape and Horseman
Vandervelde	- Seascape with Vessels
Backhuysen	- Shipping and Figures
Van der Heyden	- Country Mansion
Van der Heyden	- Cottages and Woodlands

THE FIRST FLOOR

Principal Bedrooms

The gallery overlooks the salon, on the first-floor level with bedrooms opening off it on three sides, four having corner positions, their great bays opening onto small balconies with superb views over the gardens and trees. The gallery itself is a decorative addition without any windows, but taking its light from its wide curtained arches opening onto the salon and the great dome above.

From the balconies under the arches, guests could pause to listen to the music or watch a ball or reception in the salon below. However, while leaning on the mahogany rail, few would guess that its gold and black open work, containing Alfred's monogram, is not of solid metal but merely of plaster.

On either side of the main staircase, two smaller stairs, behind glass doors, take guests to bedrooms on upper floors. In the half-moon above these glass-panelled double doors is some fine plaster-work showing seated classical females, who echo similar scenes above

the doors of other bedrooms on the same landing. Largely Greek inspired, they repeat themes of nymphs and cupids in an eternal pastoral idyll, many featuring musical instruments.

Elsewhere, on wall panels, occur delicate oval pictures in the style of Wedgewood cameos, showing classical maidens with a basket of fruit on their heads, carrying a censer, clashing cymbals or playing a triangle, while the bedroom door panels display dancing nymphs.

All these are surrounded by delicate borders which continue on both sides of the gallery and on the ceiling, with the exception of the two darkest corners furthest away from the stairways, where arch-shaped mirrors reflect borrowed light and the ceiling becomes a dome finished with gold leaf patterns. There is, however, in the wall facing the grand staircase, a large decorative door to a nonexistent room. Behind it were two bathrooms. The dummy door was evidently to give symmetry to the whole design.

The rooms opening off this fine gallery are today a disappointment. Still very high, about 14½ feet, they are now shorn

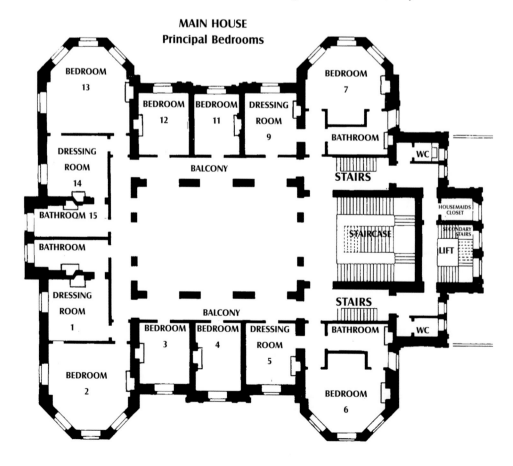

MAIN HOUSE
Principal Bedrooms

of their expensive hangings and apart from their chaste marble fireplaces, they contain little decorative plasterwork, except around the cornices. Imagination, however, can fill them with elaborate Victorian draperies, furniture and flowers, and then people them with colourful, interesting guests and scurrying valets or maidservants and you have a picture of what they may have looked like in their heyday.

This floor contained four master suites, each consisting of a bedroom, with radiator, dressing room and bathroom. Two smaller suites had a bedroom and dressing room next to one another. This can be verified by the matching cornices and fireplaces.

Of interest is the suite used by Alfred de Rothschild. If the patterns on the bedroom doors are examined, above the obligatory dancing nymphs can usually be seen a decorative motif of musical instruments, symbols of the chase or flowers. One door only carries the Rothschild arrows. This opened onto the bathroom of Alfred de Rothschild - the only unnumbered room - and indicated that his suite was, as might be expected, to the front of the house with the winter garden alongside. The bay of the Master Bedroom overlooked the south front with its lawns and trees. The red dressing room - Alfred always favoured this colour - lay between bathroom and bedroom. There is still a simple classical marble fireplace in both dressing room and bedroom.

All the bedrooms on this floor were elaborately furnished, most of the woodwork being white, with curtains and carpets in a variety of soft colours, pink or rose, green or yellow - sometimes flowered and sometimes striped in satin. Alfred's bedroom contained some finer curtains and cabinets of small collectors' pieces but the furnishings in most of the rooms were similar and equally rich.

A typical bedroom might contain a six-foot, fourposter bed of white enamel with inset painted panels and Rose du Barry silk panels, hung with festoon drapery, also in Rose du Barry silk. The window curtains would match. The bed would have an eiderdown in pink or green silk and a bedspread in silk and lace applique work. A lady's bedroom would contain more lace in the hangings.

Then there would be pieces like a wardrobe, a toilet table (dressing table), washstand and bedside tables, some with painted enamel scenes inset into the white-painted wood. Washstand and toilet table would be set with toilet or dressing sets, often two apiece, in valuable china and silver. In addition there was a settee, some easy chairs, occasional chairs upholstered in Rose du Barry satin, a writing table, two tapestry screens, a bidet, a footbath, gilt and brass ormolu electric table-lamps, clocks, potpourri vases and a few more occasional tables. Everything was in the height of luxury, but the wonder was, despite the large size of the rooms, how they could hold so much.

After all this opulence, it is almost a relief, and certainly a surprise, to find a small - room at the end of the gallery beside the main staircase, designated as Mr Hubbard's room (now a bathroom) - perhaps this was originally the missing room Number 10. This contained only one big circular table on walnut supports - probably a rent table - one or two very small tables and two chairs. As Mr Hubbard was Alfred's Halton agent, this was obviously a business room, spartan in its furnishings, but those of the very best. The linoleum was softened with a blue 'Turkey' carpet matching the blue flowered window curtains and the only decorations were two wallmounted pairs of Purdey guns. The content of the room explains much about its occupant and, incidentally, shows on what excellent terms Mr Hubbard must have remained with Alfred de Rothschild throughout his life.

At the end of the landing above the main staircase, behind two double doors alongside the ascending stairs, were two hand wash-basins and toilets, though these were only for gentlemen - ladies had commodes in their rooms. Each floor had a housemaid's closet where the Halton maidservant stored the linen and materials for cleaning, and this also stood behind the double doors and was served by a secondary stair.

THE SECOND FLOOR

Bachelor's Quarters

The second-floor corridor looked out through small close-spaced windows onto the stair light, the roof and the dome over the salon. All bedroom views, however, were of the park and gardens. The arrangement of rooms here very much resembled those on the floor beneath, with the main bedrooms in the four turrets. The two major suites had a bedroom, dressing room and a narrow bathroom, while the two smaller suites had no dressing rooms, only a bathroom. The remaining six bedrooms could, by turning a bedroom into a dressing room, share one between the two. Two of the main bathrooms were also intended to be shared by the other guests since there were no communicating doors, as on the floor below. Even the two major dressing rooms could be pressed into service as extra bedrooms, if required. Toilets and housemaid's closet were arranged as before.

The windows on this floor did not open onto outside balconies and were much smaller than those beneath, many windows being reduced to a smallish oval in the lesser bedrooms and dressing rooms. The inclusion of dormer windows also meant that, except where a room projected outwards in the plan, it had a slanting roof on the exterior wall, or in the turret bedrooms on all three sides.

As time progressed and Alfred's houseparties grew, it was necessary to bring dressing rooms into service, providing twelve bedrooms numbered 15-20 and 23-28, and since the majority of the guests were single and male, it resulted in this being dubbed the bachelors' floor.

Each bedroom had a half-tester bed with curtains matching those at the windows. The beds were made of a boxspring mattress with a wool overlay in a white cover, an underblanket, a pair of down pillows and a bolster, a pair of linen sheets, three wool blankets, a white Marcella quilt and a fairly simple

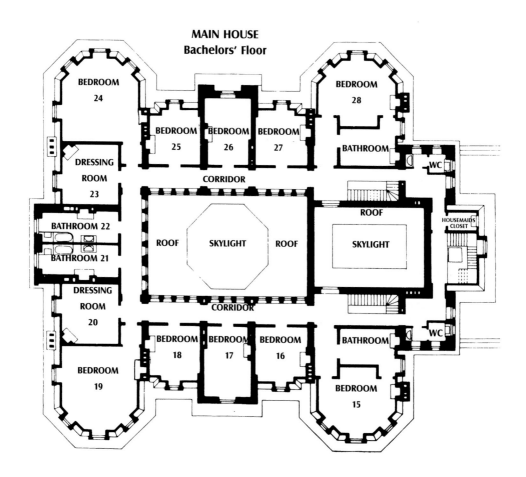

MAIN HOUSE
Bachelors' Floor

92

coverlet of silk and wool in varying colours.

The bedroom suite was of satinwood and included a large wardrobe with a central full-length mirrored door, a marble-topped washstand-set with jug, basin, soap, shaving dish and other pieces in best china, (hot water was left outside the bedroom door in a long-spouted, brass water-can) a bidet and a toilet table with a matching full set of eight china articles, including a tray, a pair of candlesticks, several round-ridded pots and dishes, brushes, combs and a tall cheval glass. There were also bedside tables, cane-seated chairs, a couch, armchairs and writing tables with their accessories including telegram forms and stamps. The room must have been literally crowded with furniture. On the walls of several of the rooms intended for specific guests were hung their favourite portraits, photographs or prints.

Bathrooms in rooms 21, 22 and two others, unnumbered, provided hip baths and commodes with the usual other furnishings, still very much of the nineteenth century, although there was a washbasin and toilet with running water at both ends of the corridor. With a maximum of twelve bedrooms on the first floor and twelve on the second, the estimation by Cecil Roth that the house could sleep up to twenty-five guests was probably not far off the mark, though he may be mistaken in assuming that dining space would be inadequate, as we know that over forty dined in the 1884 housewarming party and other photographs show it was capable of dining even more when the occasion required.

THE THIRD FLOOR

Attic Bedrooms

The attic storey with its dark rooms and slanting ceilings and up so many flights of stairs, was intended for the use of the ladies' maids and valets of any of the visiting guests.

When looking at the house from the outside, few would expect or recognise, that there was a third floor here at all. It stands on top of the house masked by some of the roofs in front. This storey, as with the ones below, could be compared to three boxes, one inside another. In the outer square are the bedrooms. The innermost square is the open expanse of roof in the middle, while in between roof and bedrooms, lies the communicating corridor. In fact, the layout is really more like a U, since one side is open. The corridor looks out onto the central roof or dome below and the belvedere or flagpole above, through small close-set, oval swing-windows, rather like portholes. Central heating and other pipes plus store cupboards are more frequent on this storey.

This floor, however, has its peculiarities. Its four turret rooms have no windows - two have plastered ceilings and two are wood-lined to the turret top. All four were therefore used for storage as box rooms. Moreover, one half of this floor was separated from the other, as in the east servants' wing, and is referred to as the north and south attic. The circular staircase to the belvedere led up internally from this storey, where it was closed in by a glass-fronted octagonal cubicle with its own entrance door.

There was still the same arrangement of toilets in each half block and there were two tiny housemaid's closets, though these no longer had any access to the secondary stairs. Provision was made for two toilets but there were no bathrooms on this floor, though two appeared next to the turret stores after the plans were first drawn.

There were five bedrooms in each of the north and south attics, each side being a mirror image of the other.

Bedroom 1, a small square room, supplied one occupant with the usual bedroom furniture and brass bedstead. It contained a small fireplace and has two small oval windows.

Bedroom 2 has a toilet and cupboard in its entrance corridor. The bedroom beyond is a smallish room with a single window. It contained in the south three beds (one folding) and in the north three normal beds, together with the usual bedroom furniture. Through the doorway behind, is the windowless multi-sided room used for storage.

MAIN HOUSE
Attic Bedrooms

NORTH

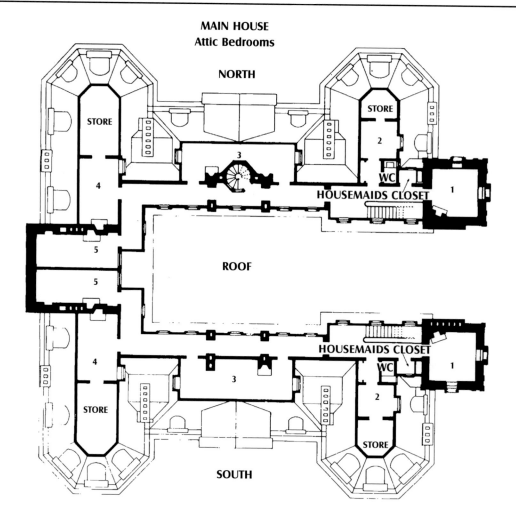

STORE

STORE

2

3

WC

4

1

HOUSEMAIDS CLOSET

5

ROOF

5

HOUSEMAIDS CLOSET

4

WC

1

3

2

STORE

STORE

SOUTH

The north **bedroom 3** is very much narrowed by the extrusion of the back of the spiral staircase to the belvedere. Since this made it so much smaller than its twin on the opposite side of the house, the north room contained, with the usual bedroom furniture, one folding and only two ordinary painted iron bedsteads, whereas the southern Bedroom 3 contained three. Both long bedrooms are lit by two small oval windows at opposite ends and have a fireplace.

Bedroom 4 with a small window and fireplace, also accommodated three beds and furniture. The turret room used for storage lies directly behind this bedroom.

Bedroom 5, the only bedroom whose window looks out over the central roof, also contained among its furnishings three beds and a fireplace. The two Bedroom 5's lay side by side but had no communicating door. The reason was that the northern rooms were for visitors' male staff, the southern for female and they were kept rigidly separate, even to the extent of using different staircases at the end of their corridors. These now have a corridor opened between them, although this gives the rooms only borrowed light.

All bedrooms, other than number 5, look outwards, though their view is restricted mainly to roofs and chimney-stacks.

The fact that these rooms are small and crowded, does not necessarily show Victorian indifference to the comfort of staff. It must be remembered that these bedrooms were only occupied for a few days, rarely more than a week, by visitors. Permanent staff had much more spacious and comfortable single rooms in their own wing.

A noteworthy feature on this attic floor is the eight fireplaces, which are small, black and late Victorian but they are set in a white marble surround, with an open gaspipe fitting, for light, above the mantelshelf.

The corridors were well supplied with firebuckets, firepumps on iron wheeled-frames and miscellaneous pieces of furniture like chairs and armchairs, including spare dining chairs.

When full, the whole attic floor could sleep twenty-four persons, twelve on the north and twelve on the south, increasing to a total of twenty-six, if the folding beds were brought into use. When numbers exceeded this accommodation, Alfred had arrangements with local hotels for taking the overflow. It is interesting to note that this frequently happened.

The Roof

The centre of the roof of both east service wing and main house was flat, leaded and broken by a dome and other glass covers or louvred fanlights to the rooms below. The main dome was supported with metal struts, having two 'skins' - layers of glass - one to protect the other, and a narrow inspection space between the two. The turrets are topped with iron rods looking like pinnacles but serving as lightning conductors. There are doors to most towers and walk-ways, again to assist inspection.

Cuffed chimney stacks of even height, surrounding turret tops and top-most roofs, ornament both back and front of the house giving a definite English touch to the continental style.

The belvedere is an architectural flight of fancy, possibly owing something to Christopher Wren's domes. It was meant not merely as decoration but to enable the visitor to see the breath-taking view from this point of eminence. Reached by a twisting stair lit by a circle of small oval windows, you come out of a small door at its base. A few more steps along the leaded pedestal on which it stands, brings you to a metal staircase guarded by metal rails. Four deep steps up and you ascend onto a platform. Around you is a stone parapet set into columns of high stone arches, which spring up and meet high above your head. These are cased in metal for extra strength.

Above is a dome, with yet another tiny arched gallery and dome, topped with the familiar pinnacle.

This is about level with the flag on the flagpole nearby. The flag rises from a decorative ironwork balustrade on the roof of its own tower, which houses built-in winding gear, enabling the pole to be winched down to within twelve feet of the roof.

The Belvedere

95

CHAPTER 9

The Grotto

THE GARDENS

"Our England is a garden that is full of stately views, of borders, beds and shrubberies and lawns and avenues, with statues on the terrace and peacocks strutting by. . . " Kipling

Alfred's gardens were judged to be pretty, even delightful, by some of his visitors, but to others, even his partial cousins at Aston Clinton, considered that though elaborate, they "might have been more advantageously laid out". In coming to a fair assessment of Alfred's achievements, several factors must be considered.

Taste in house and garden is influenced by the fashions favoured in a particular century as well as the very individual personal preferences of a creator or onlooker. Moreover, several Rothschilds have been notable in the world of gardening, so inevitably Alfred faced stiff competition. Although he loved flowers everywhere, from buttoniere to table arrangements, from flower painting to desk-top plants, Alfred was, at heart, a townsman. Halton was essentially a grand town house transported to a country setting. His preferences, therefore, were for a striking appearance and orderliness - qualities not necessarily associated with good garden planning. He spared no expense in the creation and maintenance of the gardens but favoured the formal style of gardening, more popular on the continent, together with additional spectacular features to serve his own particular interests.

TASTE IN HOUSE AND GARDEN IS INFLUENCED BY THE FASHIONS FAVOURED IN A PARTICULAR CENTURY AS WELL AS THE VERY INDIVIDUAL PERSONAL PREFERENCES OF A CREATOR OR ONLOOKER.

Appearance

He drew a definite distinction between the house-garden and park - the one firmly under control and fenced, the other being nature assisted by man. Also, since the house was built on the slope of a hill, he used this to vary garden levels with flights of steps and ornamentation in the form of urns, bowls, statues and summer houses as well as introducing peacocks and other creatures, all of which played nearly as important a part as plants. Lawns filled the gaps, acting as a well manicured, green setting to the flowers and the house, or sweeping in gentle inviting curves downhill. Trees provided the necessary contrast. Many were exotic foreign varieties giving foliage in a wide range of colours from pale green to red. The rest were supposed to include at least one example of every kind of tree found in the British Isles. These were planted in clumps to give background colour, decorate the views or mask areas not intended for display. They contained winding walks and often opened into hidden gardens. Woodlands, thick with beech, away from the house, providing cover for shooting parties. The house itself was islanded by wide paths, some curving, as on the south carriageway facing the main entrance porch, and others radiating straight out from the approximate square within which the house lay.

A wide sweeping drive from the main south door cut through trees and finally emerged onto the main road, along which Alfred planted a further avenue of trees. He had to compensate the local authority for the overuse of its roads, owing to the increased traffic caused by visitors to his new house.

Thus at the immediate back and front of the house were paths, formal flower beds and broad expanses of lawn backed by woodlands. Here could be found a Chinese Water Garden, a Grotto, an Italian Garden, several rose gardens, while certain plots contained such specialities as a Pyramid Bed, a Floral Clock, a Sundial Bed, one resembling a flower basket, as well as little plots of flowers and urns leading to the fountain at the back, or surrounding the central pedestal light in the front. Topiary even added to the spectacle alongside the drive nearest the house.

Kitchen Gardens

Many acres of kitchen gardens, sheds and orchards were on the west or further side of Halton Village beyond the cricket pavilion. The outsize cucumbers and asparagus, the rosy apples and pears that graced Alfred's tables and ran away with prizes in the annual horticultural show, were grown here and here too were the

potting sheds and nurseries. Nearby were fifty greenhouses, heated by coke fires, which provided the house plants, the exotic orchids, Alfred's favourite red carnations, perfect peaches, nectarines and grapes, the out-of-season fruit, the palms and climbers for the Winter Gardens, as well as the bedding plants for garden displays. They also produced plants for the approved lay-out of tenants' front gardens.

Bedding Table

Gardening authorities at the turn of the century equated status with the number of bedding plants in a garden.

10,000 plants denoted a squire
20,000 plants denoted a baronet
30,000 plants denoted an earl
50,000 plants denoted a duke

One of his gardeners calculated that Alfred kept over 40,000 bedding plants in his garden, showing that although technically a commoner, his standing was somewhere between an earl and a duke.

GARDEN FEATURES STILL EXISTING AT HALTON HOUSE

Special Gardens

Another of Alfred's favourite flowers was the rose. This, therefore, could be found in abundance in house and garden. One special rose garden was the Italian Garden set among the trees near

A garden party at Halton

View of Halton House from the ornamental lake

the fountain. It was entered by a pair of impressive black wrought-iron gates decorated with Alfred's monogram picked out in gold. It had a central garden, at first covered with turf broken by circular flower beds and urns.

Later it was filled with different varieties of roses, surrounded by a fine mosaic path, edged with marble and arched over at intervals with rambler roses. Surrounding the garden was a metal fence and a thick hedge cut into niches to display statues - later shrouded with covers for protection during his absences. At the furthest end was a marble-floored summer house, the front of which was closed by a type of venetian blind, which could be raised or lowered. Over the summer house was a painted dome, punctuated with five round windows in a decorative metal surround, resembling those on the top floor of the house.

Fountain

Water played an important part in the garden, as well as in the house. The centrepiece was the fountain on the north side. This was a tall, three-tiered, stone affair. Emerging from greenery at the base, were three mermaids supporting a bowl. In the middle of this bowl reared three dolphins. They held up a central column and another bowl containing three water jets. The whole fountain was really very simple when compared with the chief fountain in the gardens of other

Rothschild properties at Waddesdon or Ascott, but it attracted many compliments when the house was first opened, particularly on its appearance at night, since it was floodlit from the start, both from lights set into the waterline as well as overhead.

Lake

Another feature in the garden was the large artificial lake created some distance to the south-west of the house. Many of Alfred's garden parties were held around its edges, scattered with tasteful benches and a skating pond pavilion. This man-made lake was shallow, lined with concrete slabs and surrounded by trees, which have today encroached up to its verge, so that it is practically hidden. In the centre was a large filter and a plug for the water to be drained off. It could be filled at choice. The lake could also be used as a skating rink in winter.

Circus pony

Circus pony

Circus

Alfred's circus was another attraction in his grounds. This was one of his more eccentric pursuits, perhaps for his own pleasure but more to add to the diversions of his guests.

A circus pavilion had been created

The Swiss Chalet

beside a circular circus ring - parts are still visible today. The ring was surrounded by a high fence. Here, on suitable occasions, Alfred would entertain his visitors to a circus programme in miniature. He maintained staff and animals for the circus throughout his tenure at Halton, as well as employing special acts from home and abroad to add to its variety.

Swiss Chalet

Yet another diversion was a visit to the Swiss Chalet on the nearby hill. Although the primary function of this building was connected with the operation of the lift in the house, the Chalet was also pressed into service for the additional purpose of entertaining guests. With most of the first floor given over to water storage, it was, nevertheless, a little house complete in itself, containing a kitchen, dining room, drawing room, bedroom, dressing room and bathroom. It was designed to look like an Austrian Chalet in the Alps with a steep sloping roof, leadlined, timbered walls, a rustic wooden balcony upstairs and down, and rustling panels of green

metal ivy covering the walls. The last caretakers were Mr and Mrs Vince, who lived here with their children - Mrs Vince acting as hostess to Alfred's visitors.

Rumour whispered that Lily Langtry had once occupied the Chalet under Alfred's protection. Not only do local people vehemently deny this but Lily, not noted for her reticence, does not mention it. Besides, Alfred's visits to Halton were few, short and usually with a large company, so it seems unlikely. On

Interior of the Swiss Chalet

Interior of the Indian Pavilion

the other hand, Lily was the object of at least one of Alfred's famous "Adoration Dinners" and was a houseparty guest at Halton.

On such facts grows imagination.

Alongside was a skittles alley. This measured around 75 by 14 feet, had its own central heating and was structured of metal girders and glass. The metal framed window and roof panels, inset with heavy plate glass, were about 10 feet wide and so arranged that each one of a pair on the south side could slide on runners behind the other.

Another unusual feature was that, with the aid of a winch, the entire

Mansion Hill Lodge. Rothschild feather panel under upstairs window.

western half of the roof could be slid over the eastern part during hot summers. The pale green decorative iron roof spas, centred with the AR Monogram, were about 12 feet apart and each carried a water-cooled oil lamp, hanging from a bronze hook. Behind the skittles alley were kennels for breeding miniature spaniels. Steps were cut out of the hillside leading up to the chalet, and to this day some remain.

Summer Houses

Also in the garden were numerous summer houses, some offering simple rustic shade from the sun but others containing surprising interiors, like the Indian Pavilion. Near the previous Halton House, the boathouse was still maintained. There were also two lodges guarding the entrances to the east and west of the house, one on the opposite side of the Tring-Wendover road and the other at the end of the present McEwen Ride into Halton village. These are decorated with Rothschild plaster panels.

Cricket Pavilion

Alfred also created the cricket pavilion and grounds west of the village, still in use by the cricket team. Alfred was a keen follower of cricket matches and boasted of the prowess of the team he could field from his house staff. To be a good cricketer was a sure recommendation to find employment with Alfred. The pavilion itself was large. It housed ladies' and gentlemens' dressing rooms, a kitchen, yard and scullery, as well as the all important refreshment room. In his grounds and gardens, in the same way as in the village, Alfred displayed a curiously practical streak, since everything was present for a purpose; the trees to give vistas or to stock game, the kitchen gardens and greenhouse to supply his table with the choicest and rarest of foods and blooms, the flower beds to colour the view and his outdoor curiosities, to give guests the widest variety of entertainment that he could devise.

Gardeners

The care and upkeep of the park and garden, both kitchen and house, was under the control of the Head Gardener, who in later years was a Mr Robert Sanders. He employed 60 gardeners, among whom were Messrs. Bubb, Thirl, Field, Stevens, Cryer and Strike - all living at Halton. There was a strict hierarchy among garden staff and a clear line of training for assistants, specialisations in defined areas, movement up the ladder of experience to journeyman and then on to more responsibilities.

Most of the staff lived in Halton village, the married men in houses, the single men in a bothy on the east side of the cricket pavilion. This bothy was not quite so simple as the name implies, since it contained five bedrooms, a sitting room, a Mess Room and a Kitchen, and was therefore a kind of serviced, supervised, boarding house - nothing like as rustic a lodging as the name normally implies.

For those days pay was good - accommodation came with the job and Alfred's junior staff had a generous eight days paid annual holiday. This was an active, thriving world of its own, the work continuing with the seasons whether Alfred was there or not.

Today the gardens are only a shadow of what they once were, but at certain times from the Belvedere above the house, the outlines of vanished features can still be traced and certainly enough remains to convey an idea of what was once there. Now, simpler and more mature, the gardens still give pleasure - the main reason for their creation - and that surely was what Alfred would have wished!

Officers on the hills above Halton 1914

BEFORE THE GREAT WAR

For a time, at any rate, this district has lost touch with the army . . . Indeed the aeroplane by turning our thoughts to the heavens may give us a straighter outlook but it is certainly destroying our concentration. Bucks Herald

As the years went on, Halton saw Alfred infrequently, usually for only short periods a few times a year. Soon those in the area began to think that Alfred was immortal - rarely seen but always existing, so that life would continue unchanged under his mild and benevolent regime.

Perhaps the first crack in confidence and stability appeared when Queen Victoria died in 1901, followed in a decade by her son Edward and the coronation of her grandson George V in 1911. Already Alfred had helped the British Government during several minor foreign disasters, and being of an excessively nervous nature, he must have dreaded the possibility of War. His financial interests and his Continental family connections, however, meant that in his position he could not avoid seeing the storm clouds slowly gathering over Europe. So could the government. Preparations were stepped up and naval and army exercises were more in earnest. In 1912 and 1913 the army held its routine summer manoeuvres in the High Wycombe district.

Ironically, the 1913 manoeuvres

"THE ENGINE THROBS! IN EVERY HOUSE THE CRY GOES UP - ANOTHER ONE; DOORS BANG AND THE WHOLE VILLAGE IS IN THE STREET OR GARDEN, ABSORBED IN THE NEW PASTIME OF SKY-STARING".

presupposed a situation where two powers, formerly enemies, suddenly allied and declared war against a third, formerly their friend. The scenario of the exercise was that Greenland of the north and Brownland of the South were attacking Whiteland, lying between them. English civilians, aware also of the growing danger of war, turned out in large crowds to cheer the troops and displayed the keenest patriotism.

Alfred willingly loaned part of his Halton estate to the military. He even came to Halton himself to see what was going on, in much the same spirit as sightseers watched the battles of the Crimea and Boer Wars. Thus it was that in the week of Friday 19 September 1913, 2,500 men and 150 officers arrived at Halton Park.

Also three aircraft and an airship landed on the hill near today's Maitland Block. Anxious to make a further small contribution to manoeuvres, Alfred treated them all with lavish kindness, erecting huge marquees for their use. He called in a London caterer with a small army of chefs and waiters to feed the officers, while a local firm did the catering

The first residents of
'Halton-on-Mud'

for the men. The food was the best obtainable - Aylesbury duck, chicken, ham, tongue and roast beef. This, however, worried the army, lest the men, unaccustomed to such rich diet, might get too fat to march or fight.

Consequently, eating was restricted to one meal a day. With endearing, if rather pathetic illogic however, Alfred continued his attentions, inviting the officers to his home and entertaining them so well that the memory of such princely hospitality is still recalled with pleasure by those who enjoyed it.

Meanwhile the flying continued to the awe and delight of those in the Wendover area. Stories were told of barbers leaving customers half-shaved, while they gazed skywards; of normally brisk shop assistants going into a dream on hearing the magic roar of a passing plane, and then forgetful of customers, rushing into the street to see this phenomenon.

An old gentleman of seventy asked to be awakened from his afternoon nap "if those pesky aeroplanes flew overhead". Dinners were burned, telephone calls went unanswered.

"The engine throbs! In every house the cry goes up - another one; then it's down tools for everybody, doors bang and the whole village is in the street or garden, absorbed in the new pastime of sky-staring". (Bucks Herald)

The local news correspondent concluded that it was just as well that the army moved on at the end of the week, taking its aeroplanes with it, otherwise something like a revolution in life and habits might have been created in these sleepy little villages.

Alfred seems to have been as star-struck as his tenants. It is perhaps justice that the Royal Air Force, though regrettably in these days without its active-service aircraft, has once more returned to his estate.

CHAPTER 11

The first apprentice - A.A Akehurst

THE
ROYAL AIR
FORCE

TAKES OVER

*"The house and its surroundings are eminently suited . . .
and there is an aerodrome within a quarter of a mile."* 1919 Lord Trenchard

THE 'FATHER'

OF THE ROYAL

AIR FORCE,

LORD

TRENCHARD,

QUICKLY SEIZED

ON THIS

OPPORTUNITY

TO

INCORPORATE

THE EXISTING

FACILITIES AT

HALTON INTO

THE ROYAL AIR

FORCE

In the last two years before the War, Alfred went into a frenzy of entertaining, perhaps knowing or fearing that time was running out for him and his way of life. He spent even more lavishly - over £2,000 for entertainment on one houseparty. In the same year as the manoeuvres, Sir Lauder Brunton stayed with him, as well as Mr Charles Davis and Mischa Elman, with only one lady present among those visitors. At another weekend Madame Melba was one of the guests.

Alfred's last big Halton houseparty was held in July 1914; August 1914 saw the outbreak of the First World War. Having struggled so hard and so long to help prevent it, Alfred was devastated. Not only did it damage the world of finance in which he moved but it was a personal disaster, catching many of his closely knit but scattered family on opposing sides, some branches never really recovering afterwards.

Eager to help, Alfred offered his Halton Estate to the army. His great friend was Lord Kitchener and patriotically Alfred sought to put at his disposal whatever could shorten the forthcoming cataclysm. His offer was taken up and, shortly, at the end of 1914, army units appeared under training at Halton Park as well as in nearby Aston Clinton. At a stroke the old life crumbled and disappeared. Thus

Halton Park was utilised by the infantry, first as an overflow from Aldershot for training and then for interservice engineering training. Vast areas bristled with tents and all kinds of buildings. Much of the technical training for aircraft personnel became centred here, to such an extent that in the Summer of 1917 the School of Technical Training eventually emerged to train mechanics as fitters and riggers for the Royal Flying Corps, and in due course, on the 1st April 1918, for the Royal Air Force. This change necessitated replacing tents with permanent buildings of huts and workshops, while heavy, expensive engineering equipment was brought in. Lieutenant Colonel Bonham Carter was the first Officer to command the School. In 1919 the first Hospital was also set up at Halton.

One more gesture Alfred made, offering his glorious beeches, by now approaching full growth, to the Timber Control Board to be used as props in the waterlogged trenches of the battle areas of Europe. Again the offer was accepted and the woods laid low. Today's plantation of firs are later replacements. A similar fate overtook many trees so painstakingly cultivated in the garden. A skeleton staff still maintained the house, as Alfred was still paying them during the war, but many on the Estate joined up - strangely Alfred never forgave them this. Gradually

Lord Trenchard inspects the apprentices at Halton

*The new Halton Camp
arises*

everything ran down, ditches blocked, undergrowth running riot, gardens neglected and boundaries undefined. The Mansion itself stood shuttered and isolated; outgrown by the war and the busy camp below it - a ghost from a dream of peace - its treasures in storage, its furniture hidden under heavy covers. This transformation must have grieved Alfred as much as the continuation of the War. There were no more house-parties and hardly any more visits to Halton.

Alfred's health, under increasing strain, began to fail. Never a strong man, he nevertheless outlived his brothers, who died in 1915 and 1917, leaving him with more responsibility and less support. Lord Kitchener's death was another severe personal blow, and deaths in action of family and friends isolated him still more. He remained working at the bank, now well into his seventies, but he had lost his interest and enjoyment in living.

Times were changing and he no longer could keep up with them, sick and tired as he was. His death in January 1918, after a short illness ending in pneumonia, came as little surprise to those who knew him. Alfred, having held the stage for so long, knew the right time to leave gracefully. He was 75.

In his will he remembered his family, his many friends and those who had served him, with typical generosity. The house and furnishings, the painting and art works, which he had so loved and painstakingly collected, were dispersed or sold. An era had disappeared.

Halton House and its estate passed to his nephew, Mr Lionel Nathan de Rothschild, because "he was the only Rothschild without a country house". Alas, Lionel did not like the place, the final blow being when he found the soil wrong for growing rhododendrons - by such apparently insignificant features the course of history is changed! He, having his eye on another property at Exbury in Hampshire, and having first emptied Halton house in a grand sale in August 1918, after much bargaining sold the whole estate to the fledgling Royal Air Force for the nominal sum of £112,000 (its probate value was around £360,000) incidentally, saving the War Office vast sums in reparation. The 'Father' of the Royal Air Force, Lord Trenchard, quickly seized on this opportunity to incorporate the existing facilities at Halton into his reorganisation of the Royal Air Force, since engineering training and flying had continued at Halton in a diminished form but without a break. In March 1920, he inaugurated a new Apprentice Scheme for aircraft engineering trades

The Billiard Room converted to an Ante Room, Halton House Officers' Mess 1920

Main Staircase 1920

room has also changed its function and, in so doing, most of the older wall decoration has disappeared, though the ceiling remains intact. The billiard table - the only original article of furniture to remain in the house - has also seen some moves, during which the slate base was cracked in two. This, now repaired and expensively restored to its pristine condition, has been moved. Some of the fireplaces have changed and many have been blocked up. Nevertheless, the downstairs public rooms of the main house and the upstairs bedrooms still remain in use, much as they were in Alfred's day.

There are three major new additions. Corridors have been created joining the main house to the service wing and the dividing walls on the top floors removed.

In 1937 the single Officers' quarters of the West Wing replaced the Winter Garden, which had been finally pulled down in 1935. The new stone building in the shape of a hollow square was cleverly integrated to blend in with existing architecture. This three-storey addition was mainly intended for bed and sitting room suites for officers, and originally contained twelve double and twenty-seven single rooms, but as time passed, more rooms have been used as single rooms to allow larger numbers to be accommodated.

Stewards employed in the Mess during

and in 1922 apprentices in mechanical trades started training at Halton, where they have since remained alongside the hospital. A large part of the remaining estate, has, over the years, been sold.

In 1919, Halton House became the Officers' Mess of Royal Air Force Halton, the house and grounds partly refurbished by the efforts of German prisoners of war, the main house providing the public rooms.

A present-day visitor will notice that the wall between the garden entrance and the boudoir has been replaced by an arch, thus creating a much larger room. In the same way the room used by Alfred as a library, the last surviving room hung with gold silk, is now a store room, though the fine ceiling, fireplace and bookcases are still in place. The dining

the 1950s found themselves accommodated in the old servants' quarters on the hidden third floor. Numerous pranks were played on fellow stewards and officers alike and good use was made of the Belvedere to send signals to the Nurses' quarters on the distant hospital site. Eventually it was decided that, for the peace of mind and privacy of officers, the mess staff would be moved to the main camp accommodation, meaning a long and sometimes cold walk to and from work.

The kitchens have been modernised several times in their history but a large, flatroofed, one-storey dining room was eventually added in 1960, alongside the north wall of the kitchens.

Spiritual Residents

In a house aged a hundred or so years, it is almost expected for it to acquire a resident ghost or two, particularly when, as in this case, its interior recalls the eighteenth rather than the nineteenth-century. A few stories are in circulation to which it is somewhat difficult to give a more mundane explanation. Out of interest, here are a few.

The Chinese landing takes its name from a Chinese servant. The Chinaman wore white, did not speak and was often seen ironing his master's clothes in the corridor outside his bedroom in the service wing, where one day he was found hanged. It seems, however, that he still continues his ironing when the spirit moves him!

Guests to the Summer Ball or Christmas Draw have also commented on meeting a stranger, in a very decolleté dress of an earlier period, walking up the top flight of the grand staircase and disappearing into the nearest corner bedroom of the gallery. Once, concerned when she did not emerge, a guest went in search of her, but the bedroom was empty.

Station Orderly Officers are maybe apprehensive but pretty down to earth. Several in the past have reported seeing an army officer in full "dining-in" kit which, with medals, resembles the dress of the 1st World War period, though this does not tally with the history of the

Jock Scotland, Steward at Halton House Officers' Mess 1954

house. At the time when the Orderly Officers' Room was Number 11 on the gallery, this gentleman was wont to open the door to their room and walk across it, looking neither to left nor right. Obviously very worried and pre-occupied, he finally opened the French windows and disappeared outside - causing no little concern.

Nevertheless, ghosts and structural alterations apart, also despite Service furnishings and blue uniforms replacing Victoriana, the building today is still recognisable as the one where Alfred Charles de Rothschild holidayed.

Indeed, the building still retains connections to the arts by regularly appearing on television and in film. It is a popular location for many film companies, and has played host to Meryl Streep, Sir Lawrence Olivier, Madonna, Rod Stewart and James Bond to name just a few. The Salon has been converted into a restaurant, a casino, a ballroom and a German hotel lobby. Alfred would have approved of the regular visits by A-list celebrities.

If he could still see it, he might be surprised - but perhaps not disappointed, particularly on those nights of the Mess Balls when ladies come sweeping down the grand staircase in their long dresses to dance in the grand salon under the blazing chandelier, while the fountain plays in the floodlit garden beyond . . .

HALTON HOUSE PAINTINGS

List of art works, known to have been at Halton House c1884-1918

BACKHUYSDEN	Coast Scene with Fishing Boats and Figures . . . . .(L)
	Coast Scene with Shipping . . . .(B)
BERGHEM	Landscape, Cattle and Figures . . . .(L) (SD)
	Musical Peasants . . . .(R)
BOUCHER	Girl with Pigeons crossing Stream . . . .(B)
	Cupid disarmed by Venus . . . .(SL)(A)(G)
	Venus caressing Cupid . . . .(SL)(A)(G)
	Toilet of Venus . . . .(SL)(A)(G)
	Triumph of Venus . . . .(SL)(A)(G)
BRONZINO	Young Italian Nobleman . . . .(SM)
CHAMPAIGNE	Cardinal Richelieu . . . .(R)
CUYP	Dutch Skating Scene . . . .(B)
	Flight into Egypt . . . .(D)
	Watering Place . . . .(D)
	Self Portrait . . . .(D)
	Castle with Peasants . . . .(L)
	Landscape with Hills, River and Figures . . . .(ND)
	Landscape with Castle, River and Figures . . . . . .(ND)
DOMENICHINO	Magdelen . . . .(ND)
DROUAIS	Mademoiselle Dutet . . . .(B)
(VAN) DYKE	Duchess of Richmond in Satin with Cupids . . . . .(BR)
GAINSBOROUGH	Ann Ford, Mrs Thicknesse . . . .(B)
	Mrs William Villebois . . . .(ND)
GREUZE	Polish Lady with Fur . . . .(B)
	Le Baiser Envoyer . . . .
(VAN DER) HEYDEN	Cottages and Woodland . . . .(B)
	Country Mansion . . . .(B)
	Exterior Building and Figures . . . .(L)
(DE) HOOCH	Two Gentlemen Drinking., ...(L)
HOPPNER	Mary, Duchess of Gloucester . . . .(B)

(VAN) HUYSUM	Flowers (2)	(ND)
	Flowers and Fruit (4)	(A)
JORDAENS	Portrait of a Man	(BR)
LANCRET	The Minuet	(SD)
	Garden Scene with Fountain and Figures	(SD)
	A Skating Party	(B)
	A Garden Scene with Figures	(B)
	River View with Figures	(B)
	French Garden Scene and Fruit Gathering	(B)
LAWRENCE	Lady Templeton	(SD)
MIERIS	A Music Lesson (on copper)	(L)
	A Musical Party	(L)
MURILLO	St Joseph and Infant Christ	(SM)
NETSCHER	Lady in Cream and Blue Satin Dress	(L)
	Lady in Satin Dress and seated at a Table	(SD)
OSTADE A	Villagers Dancing	(L)
OSTADE J	Exterior and Figures	(L)
	Fruit Stall	(L)
PATER	La Danse	(ND)
	Peace	(ND)
	War	(ND)
	Plaisir Champetres	(SD)
	Repos dans le Parc	(SD)
	Les Amants Heureux	(SD)
	Landscape and Figures	(B)
	Garden Scene and Figures (2)	(SD)
	Landscape and Groups of figures (2)	(B)
POTTER	Castle and Homestead	(SD)
PYNAKER	Landscape, Cattle and Figures	(SD)
RAOUX	Madame Elizabeth	(BR)
REMBRANDT	$^3/_4$ length portrait of Dutch Lady with ruff	(SD)
	$^3/_4$ length portrait of a Gentleman with lace collar and broad brimmed hat	(SD)
	Figures in Landscape	(SM)
RUBENS	Rape of the Sabines	(L)
	Figure Subject	(L)
REYNOLDS	Mary Isabella, Duchess of Rutland	(ND)
	Miss Angelo	(B)
	Lady Bamfylde	(D) (ND)

ROMNEY	Mrs Tickell . . . .(B)
	Lady Hamilton Dressed as Circe . . . .(R)
	Lady Hamilton in Morning Dress . . . .(R)
	Catherine, Lady Paulett . . . .(R)
	Mrs Webster . . . .(ND)

RUYSDAEL Landscape . . . .(L)

SNYDERS The Boar Hunt . . . .(Entrance Hall)

| STEEN J | Dutch Street and Figures . . . .(B) |
| | Village Wedding . . . .(B) |

TENIERS	Interior of a Picture Gallery . . . .(L)
	A Village Festival/Feast . . . .(R)
	Village Peasants Dancing . . . .(B)
	Exterior and Figures . . . .(L)
	Card Party . . . .(L)

TERBORCH Guitar Lesson . . . .(L)

(VAN DE) VELDE	Traveller and two Beggars . . . .(L)
	Piping Herdsman . . . .(L)
	Cattle with Shepherd and Shepheerdess . . . .(SD)
	Seascape with Vessels . . . .(B)

WATTEAU	Buildings, Garden Scene and Figures . . . .(SD)
	Garden Scene with Fountain and Figures . . . . . .(SD)
	La Fontaine . . . .(SD)

WOUVERMAN	Hawking Party (2) . . . .(SD)
	Soldiers Gambling . . . .(SD)
	Landscape with Horsemen and Figures . . . .(SD)
	Landscape with Horsemen . . . .(B)
	Return of Shooting Party . . . .(SD)
	Horsemen and Figures . . . .(SD)
	Camp Scene and Horsemen . . . .(L)

WYNANTS	Landscape . . . .(BR)
	Interior of Artist's Studio with Artist . . . .(L)
	Landscape, Figures and Hawks . . . .(L)

KEY TO LOCATIONS

NB: Paintings were often moved, from room to room or even from house to house, during Alfred de Rothschild's lifetime.

A	- Ante Room	ND	- North Drawing Room
B	- Boudoir	SD	- South Drawing Room
BR	- Billiard Room	SL	- Salon
D	- Dining Room	SM	- Smoking Room
G	- Garden Entrance	R	- Red Room
L	- Library		

Solicitors notification of the death of

Alfred Charles de Rothschild

DEATH ON OR AFTER 1st JANUARY, 1898.

Will

BE IT KNOWN that *Alfred Charles de Rothschild of Mews Court St Swithin's Lane in the*

City of London and of 1. Seamore Place in the County of Middlesex and of Halton in the

County of Buckingham died on the 31st day of January 1918 at 1 Seamore Place

aforesaid AND BE IT FURTHER KNOWN that at the date hereunder written the last Will and

Testament

of the said deceased was proved and registered in the Principle Probate Registry of His

Majesty's High Court of Justice, and that administration of the estate which by law devolves to

and vests in the personal representative of the said deceased was granted by the aforesaid Court

to *Sir Milsom Rees of 18 Upper Wimpole Street in the County of Middlesex PVD Sir Edward*

Marshall Hall of 3 Temple Gardens in the City of London Knight Barry Willicombe Mason of 2

Birchin Lane in the said City Esquire and Charles Allard Jones of New Court aforesaid Esquire the

executors

named in the said *Will*

Resources £2494024-17-11

Dated the *2nd* day of *March* 1918

Value of Estate *£1,500,000*

This grant issued in duplicate

THE LAST WILL

    This is the last will of me ALFRED CHARLES DE ROTHSCHILD of New Court, St Swithins Lane in the City of London Esquire.

    1. I appoint Sir Milsom Rees, CVO FRCS of 18 Upper Wimpole Street London W. Sir Edward Marshall Hall KC MP of 3 Temple Gardens London E.C. Barry Willicombe Mason of 2 Birchin Lane London E.C. and Charles Allard Jones of New Court aforesaid (who and the survivor of them or other the trustees or trustee for the time being hereof are hereinafter called "my Trustees") to be EXECUTORS of this my will and TRUSTEES thereof for all purposes including those of the Settled Land Acts.

    2. I make the following specific bequests free of all duties which may be payable immediately on my death videlicet:

To my sister-in-law Lady Rothschild	The picture "Le Baiser Envoyer" by Greuze
To my sister-in-law Marie de Rothschild	The portrait of Mrs Tickell by Romney in the Red Room at Seamore Place and Marriage of Teniers in Green Room at Seamore Place.
To Mrs Behrens	The round Sèvres table under picture by Cuyp in Green Room at Seamore Place.
To The Honourable Mrs Charles Rothschild	The oval Sèvres table also under picture by Cuyp in Green Room at Seamore Place.
To Almina Countess of Carnarvon	The small picture by Watteau in Red Room at Seamore Place. The three turquoise light blue Sèvres vases on piece of furniture under Tenniers in Green Room at Seamore Place. Portrait of Emma Hart by Romney in Green Room at Seamore Place. Picture of young girl by Greuze in Red Room at Seamore Place. Two small pictures by Cuyp on either side of the picture of the Marriage of Tenniers. The upright piece of furniture with Sèvres plaque in centre and the two pieces of furniture on either side underneath picture of Emma Hart all in Green Room at Seamore Place. The two Vitrines on each side of Fire Place in Red Room at Seamore Place and the contents of same except the Raphael Missel, the Green Sèvres commode and two green Sèvres tables to match the three blue Sèvres vases on the mantelpiece and the pair of tall blue lights with candles in them. The two frames on either side of the mantel piece containing miniatures on one side by Boucher and on the other by various English artists. The picture by Giorgione and the picture by Belline together with the plaque in a frame underneath which are on a narrow wall by the window near the picture by Teniers, all of which are in the Green Room at Seamore Place and also my scrap book and I express the hope that she will regard them all as heirlooms.
To Lady Ripon	The two turquoise Sèvres eventails at Halton.
To Lady Alington	The Sèvres clock with portrait of Lady on top in Red Room at Seamore Place.
To National Gallery	The picture of Lady Bamfylde by Sir Joshua Reynolds on condition it is placed and remains in a favourable position in the Building in Trafalgar Square and is not removed therefrom.

To Lady Curson	The three blue Sèvres vases (eventail shape) and small upright Sèvres cabinet in Boudoir at Halton. The portrait of Miss Angelo by Sir Joshua Reynolds in Boudoir at Halton. The two small Greuze Heads in Green Room at Seamore Place. The picture by Boucher of Girl crossing street with Pigeons in Boudoir at Halton and the three green vases (eventail shape) in Green Room at Seamore Place.
To The Earl of Carnarvon	The Raphael Missel and I express the hope that he will regard it strictly as an heirloom.
To Lady Rocksavage	The portrait of Polish Lady with Fur by Greuze in Boudoir at Halton. The three pink Sèvres Rose du Barry vases in Green Room at Seamore Place.
To Miss Alice de Rothschild	The Sèvres side table in Boudoir at Halton.
To Madame Ephrussi	The Louis XVI Ormulu and enamel clock in Hall at Halton.
To Baroness Edmond de Rothschild	Pair of small turquoise blue Sèvres vases in Boudoir at Halton.
To Baron Maurice de Rothschild	The oval Louis XVI table by David de Louisville in Bamfield Room at Halton.
To Baroness Henry de Rothschild	The tapestry fires screen in Bamfield Room at Halton.
To Baron Lambert of Brussels	The picture by Wolverman under Adrian Vandervelt in Lawrence Room at Halton.
To The Countess of Gosford	Pair of Sèvres garde a vous at Seamore Place.
To The Lady Battersea	The Battersea enamel etui at Seamore Place.
To The Honourable Mrs Eliot Yorke	The Louis XVI clock in Sèvres vase-shaped case in Boudoir at Halton.
To Sir E. Marshal-Hall	My snuffbox at Seamore Place.
To Sir Milsom Rees	Pair of Sèvres vases and clock in vase-shaped case on Louis XVI Cabinet in front of Watteau in Lawrence Room at Halton.
To Sir Milsom Rees' daughter	Pair of small blue vases on table in Sitting Room at Seamore Place.
To Sir Milsom Rees' son	My walking stick entirely of tortoiseshell at Seamore Place and my pair of Purdey Guns.
To Sir V. Caillard	The Chinese powder blue arm mounted ormulu in Sitting Room at Seamore Place.
To W. Koch	Pair of Sèvres turquoise jardinieres in Boudoir at Halton.
To Lady Brougham and Vaux	Pair of Sèvres jardinieres dark blue and green in Green Room at Seamore Place.
To Mrs Bischoffsheim	One green Sèvres jardiniere in Green Room at Seamore Place. The Louis XV or Louis XVI clock representing a lion with its foot on a golden ball in the Boudoir at Halton.
To The Earl of Ripon	My walking stick with bloodstone knob monogram in gold at Seamore Place.

To Sir Guy Laking Baronet	Twenty two Chinese objects in case in Billiard Room at Halton also Malacca stick with diamond monogram (Lord Carnarvon's) at Seamore Place
To Sir Philip Sassoon Baronet	The picture by Velasquez at Seamore Place.
To The Lady Egerton	The picture of the Duchess of Gloucester by Hoppner in Boudoir at Halton.
To Sir George Arthur Baronet	The Louis XVI clock in Telephone Room at Seamore Place.
To Lady Arthur	The Louis XVI lights at Seamore Place.
To The Marquis de Soverai	The blue Chinese Beaker with fine Louis XVI mounts in Sitting Room at Seamore Place.
To Sir Ernest Cassel Baronet	Pair of Louis XVI lights in Hall in Halton.
To Feliz Joubert	The Rock Crystal Dagger in Boudoir at Halton.
To The Lady Kilmoray	Pair of Green Sèvres jardiniere in Lawrence Room at Halton.
To The Lady Tweeddale	Vernis Martin fire-screen in Boudoir at Halton.
To The Earl Lonsdale	The tall light blue oriental vase in the Salon at Halton and on the table nearest to the Boudoir.
To Georgina Countess of Dudley	The Louis XVI jardiniere mounted on table in Telephone Room at Seamore Place.
To Minnie Lady Paget	Three Sèvres vases dark blue ground in Red Room at Halton.
To The Lord Bertie	Pair mounted Chinese vases in Billiard Room at Halton.
To Mrs Asquith	Pair of Chelsea vases in Boudoir at Halton.
To Colonel and Mrs Fludyer	The Battersea Box in Lawrence Room at Halton.
To The Honourable George Keppel	Pair of Chinese jardinieres Louis XV mounts Mrs in Sitting Room in Seamore Place.
To Lady Luking	The pink Chelsea inkstand in Boudoir at Halton.
To Mr F.W. Lee	My Malacca stick blue enamel handle at Seamore Place.
To Mrs Lee	Pair Louis XVI blue glass vases in Sitting Room at Seamore Place.
To G.F.W. Laking	My Ivory stick blue enamel handle at Seamore Place
To H.H.Trodd	All the furniture, clock and lights in the Red Dressing Room at Halton.
To F. Hubbard	Three powder blue vases in outer Hall at Halton.
To Mrs Baker	Two cylindrical Chinese turquoise vases in Green Room at Seamore Place.
To Parry	The Louis XVI clock in Red Room at Halton.
To Bennett	The picture of Wynants in Billiard Room (on sofa) at Halton.
To Mrs Cobbold	The inkstand with corals in Bedroom at Seamore Place.

To A. Crockett	My bloodstone head stick with diamonds at Seamore Place.
To George White	My gold handle horn stick. at Seamore Place.
To Lady Evelyn Herbert	The French Bureau opposite fire-place under Velasquez in Telephone Room Seamore Place.
To Lord Porchester	My Cats Eye Pin.
To Mrs Vince	Pair of Dresden Dogs in Sitting Room at Seamore Place.
To Miss Laking	The small amber clock at Seamore Place.
To Viscount Chaplin	The empire inkstand in Red Room at Halton.
To The Marquis of Lincolnshire	The Louis XVI Column clock in Red Room at Seamore Place.
To Lady Carl Meyer	The little Sèvres table close to the picture of a man by Rembrandt in Lawrence Room at Halton.
To Baroness Edward de Rothschild	The little Sèvres table close to the picture of a woman by Rembrandt in Lawrence Room at Halton.
To Lady Rees	The Elizabethan mirror in Bamfield Room at Halton.
To Baron Maurice de Rothschild	The oval inlaid table in front of mosaic table in Bamfield Room at Halton.
To Georgiana Susan Lady de Cane	The round table with Sèvres top on the left of fire-place in the Library at Halton.
To Mrs Arthur Sassoon	The round table with Sèvres top on the right of fire-place in the Library at Halton.
To Madame von Houbrouck	The pair of fans on each side of the fire-place in the Red Room at Seamore Place.
To Barry W. Mason	My walking stick with tortoiseshell knobmonogram in gold at Seamore Place.

As Sir Guy Laking is well acquainted with all the specific gifts above mentioned and has been good enough to say that he will be prepared to assist my executors in every way I express the wish that my executors will avail themselves of his help and assistance in identifying the same (if necessary) and in seeing that all the articles are carefully packed and delivered to the various beneficiaries.

3. I desire to state that it is my intention to place in cases various small articles and trinkets which I wish my executors to hand to Lady Carnarvon for her own use absolutely and so that if she so desires she may give any one or more of them to such person or persons as she may think will value same, I also direct my executors to hand over to Lady Carnarvon all my clothing and wearing apparel to be disposed of by her in such manner as she shall think fit.

4. I give and devise my freehold Mansion House Park farm and lands comprising and known as the Halton Estate to my nephew Lionel Nathan de Rothschild, the eldest son of my late brother Leopold for his life without impeachment of waste and after his death. I give and devise the said Halton Estate to the eldest of only son of the said Lionel Nathan de Rothschild and the issue of such eldest or only son in tail male with reminder to the second and other sons of the said Lionel Nathan de Rothschild successively accordingly to seniority in tail male and if the said Lionel Nathan de Rothschild shall have no son who or whose issue shall attain an interest as aforesaid in the said Halton Estate then I give and devise the said Halton Estate to my nephew Evelyn Achille de Rothschild and the issue of such eldest or only son in tail male with remainder to the second and other sons of the said Evelyn Achille de Rothschild successively accordingly to seniority in tail male and if the said Evelyn Achille de Rothschild shall have no son who or whose issue shall attain an interest as aforesaid in the said Halton Estate then I give and devise the said Halton Estate to my nephew Anthony Gustave de Rothschild the third son of my said brother Leopold for his life without impeachment of waste and after his death I give and devise the said Halton Estate to the eldest or only son of the said Anthony Gustave de Rothschild in tail male with remainder to the second and other sons of the said Anthony Gustave de Rothschild

successively and according to seniority in tail male. I give and devise all the pictures, Sèvres china, clocks, bronzes, wall and other lights, sèvres and other cabinets, curiosities and articles of vertu (except such as are by this my will or any codicil hereto specifically bequeathed) which shall at the time of my death be in or about my Mansion House, Halton aforesaid to the person who is for the time being entitled to the use and enjoyment of the said Halton Estate as heirlooms and so that the same shall devolve with the said Halton Estate and be held subject to the limitations herein before declared concerning the said Halton Estate. I give to my trustees the sum of twenty five thousand pounds free of duty upon trust to invest the same in any security or mode of investment by law permitted to trustees with power of variation or transposition and upon further trust to pay the income arising therefrom to the person for the time being entitled to the use and enjoyment of the said Halton Estate. My wish and intention being that the said income shall be applied for the maintenance and upkeep of the said Halton Estate and that the said capital sum of twenty five thousand pounds and the investments from time to time representing the same shall so far as is practicable devolve with the said Halton Estate and be held subject to the same limitations as are hereinbefore declared concerning the said Halton Estate.

5. I give and devise my freehold house No 1 Seamore Place Mayfair and the stabling held therewith to Almina, Countess of Carnarvon absolutely free of duty, I also give and bequeath to Almina, Countess of Carnarvon absolutely free of all duties payable immediately on my death all the pictures, Sèvres china, clocks, bronzes, wall and other lights, Sèvres and other cabinets, curiosities and articles or vertu, together with all the furniture and contents (except money and securities for money and except such articles as are by this m.y will or any codicil hereto specifically bequeathed to others but in addition to those specifically bequeathed to her personally) which shall at the time of my death be in and about my said house No 1 Seamore Place aforesaid and the said stabling.

6. I bequeath the following pecuniary legacies free of duty viz -

To Almina, Countess of Carnarvon	Fifty thousand pounds
To the Earl of Carnarvon	Twenty five thousand pounds
To Lord Porchester	Twenty five thousand pounds
To Lady Evelyn Herbert	Twenty five thousand pounds
To my nephew Evelyn Achille de Rothschild	Twenty five thousand pounds
To my nephew Anthony Gustav de Rothschild	Twenty five thousand pounds
To the two sons now living of Lady Curzon	Ten thousand pounds each
To the daughter now living of Lady Curzon	Five thousand pounds

And I direct that if any or either of the last three named legatees shall be under the age of twenty one years at the time of my death my executors shall pay his or her legacy to Lady Curzon who shall have the sole control thereof until such legatee attains the age of twenty one years and whose receipt shall be a sufficient discharge to my executors.

To Mme von Houbrouck	Four thousand pounds
To Lady Egerton of Tatton	Five hundred pounds
To Sir George Arthur	Five thousand pounds
To the Marquis de Several	Two thousand pounds
To Gaston Foa	Two thousand pounds
To Dr Fuller	One thousand pounds
To Sir Milsom Rees	Five thousand pounds
To Frederick Hubbard	Five thousand pounds
To C. Gibbs	One thousand pounds
To Crockett	Two thousand pounds
To Trodd my Butler at Halton	Three thousand pounds

To Lady Ripon	Five hundred pounds
To Sir Carl Meyer	Five hundred pounds
To J. Arthur Dawes	Five thousand pounds
To each of the three sons of the late Charles Davies	One thousand pounds
To Mrs Lindermann	One thousand pounds
To Parry	Three thousand pounds
To Potter	Two thousand pounds
To Sir Guy Laking	Five thousand pounds
To Mr Ashton of New Bond Street	Five hundred pounds
To Barry W. Mason	Ten thousand pounds
To C. Allard Jones	Five thousand pounds
To W. Price	Two thousand pounds
To F.W.Lee	Three thousand pounds
To Budd	Five hundred pounds
To F. Joubert	Five thousand pounds
To Sir E.Marshall Hall	Five thousand pounds
To James Willam Williams	Three thousand pounds
To George H. Tite	One thousand pounds
To Lord Esher	One thousand pounds
To Colonel Swaine	Two thousand pounds
To Howard Corbold and Clement Cooper (of New Court)	Five hundred pounds each
To Edward Barnaby (Butler at New Court)	One hundred pounds
To Ellward (Porter at New Court)	Fifty pounds
To every other porter and messenger at New Court indoor and outdoor	Ten pounds each
To Mrs Ferguson my Housekeeper	Five hundred pounds
To Bennett my Butler	Five hundred pounds
To George King my Coachman	One thousand pounds
To Jeffreys my Chauffeur	Five hundred pounds
To Rolf my servant	Five hundred pounds
To Jack Hubbard	Five hundred pounds
To George Heels and William Frith who have been in my employ at Halton for some years	Two hundred pounds each.

7. I declare that the covenant which I entered on the marriage of the Earl and Countess of Carnarvon for the payment of five hundred thousand pounds to the trustees of their Marriage Settlement remain in full force and effect and I direct and declare that the legacy hereby given to the Countess of Carnarvon and the legacies given to members of the Carnarvon family shall be paid in priority to all others.

8. Being desirous of doing honour to the name of the late Lord Kitchener of Khartoum I bequeath free of duty to the Lord Kitchener National Memorial Fund the sum of twenty five thousand pounds towards the purposes and objects of any scheme which may be in force at my death and I declare that the receipt of the Treasurer or Trustees for the time being of the said fund shall be a sufficient discharge for the same.

9. I give free of duty to Sir Bertrand Dawson KCVO MD twenty five thousand pounds for the benefit and purpose of a scheme which he has propounded to me and to Sir Wilson Rees but in the event of the said scheme not maturing the said sum shall fall into and form part of my residuary estate.

10. I give to my trustees the sum of one thousand pounds free of duty upon trust to distribute five hundred pounds part thereof as they in their absolute and uncontrolled discretion shall think fit amongst my servants both indoor and outdoor at Seamore Place (other than those to whom I have pecuniary legacies direct) and to distribute five hundred pounds balance thereof as they in their absolute and uncontrolled discretion shall think fit amongst my servants both indoor and outdoor at Halton (other than those to whom I have pecuniary legacies direct)

11. I give all the residue of my estate and effects of what nature or kind so ever including any property over which I have any general power of appointment unto my trustees upon trust to convert the same into money and after paying thereout my funeral and testamentary expenses and debts and the legacies hereby or by any codicil hereto bequeathed to distribute the same amongst such Jewish and Christian Charities in such manner and in such sums as my trustees shall in their absolute and uncontrolled discretion think fit which would no doubt include the leading London hospitals.

12. I declare that my executors and trustees may if they think fit instead of acting personally employ and pay a solicitor or any other person to transact any business or do any act required to be done in the administration of my estate or the execution of the trusts of my will and that any executor or trustee hereunder being a solicitor or other person engaged in any profession or business may be so employed to act and shall be entitled to charge all professional and other charges for any business or out done by him or his firm in connection with the executorship or trust (in addition to any legacy bequeathed to him personally) including any act which an executor or trustee not being a solicitor or other person engaged as aforesaid could have done personally.

13. I revoke all previous wills and codicils and declare this to be my last and only will AS WITNESS my hand to this my will contained in this and the nine preceding sheets of paper this eighteenth day of September One thousand nine hundred and seventeen - ALFRED C DE ROTHSCHILD - Signed by the said Alfred Charles de Rothschild in our presence we both being present at the same time and witnessed and subscribed by us in his presence. - JOSEPH HARRIS - A C GRANT Clerks to Messrs Dawes & Sons 2 Birchin Lane London E.C. Solrs. On the 2nd day of March 1918 Probate of this will was granted to Sir Milsom Rees, Sir Edward Marshall Hall, Barry Willicombe Mason and Charles Allard Jones the executors.

Acknowledgements (Third Edition)

The Historians of Halton House Officers' Mess are grateful for the kind assistance of many who have donated their time, resources and expertise in assisting with this third edition of The Story of Halton House.

Squadron Leader Beryl Escott kindly allowed us the freedom to do as we saw fit with this new edition, but few changes were required to her fresh and inspiring text. We are grateful for the support of the Rothschild Archive Trust, and especially that of the Senior Archivist, Melanie Aspey. The curators and guides at Waddesdon Manor have also allowed us into their archives, and among many local personalities who have visited Halton House, we were privileged to meet and speak with the late Jock Scotland. Our thanks go to his widow Irene and the family for permission to reproduce his pictures here. Mike Bass and Jill Fowler of Lime Tree Studios in Tring have allowed us access to their collection of local memorabilia and the Bucks Herald has kindly permitted the use of some of their photographs of Halton House. The curators of both the Trenchard Museum at Royal Air Force Halton and The Walter Rothschild Museum in Tring have given us great licence to view their collections and assist our research. Finally, our grateful thanks go to Group Captain (Ret'd) Min Larkin who has always made himself available to answer our questions and correct our misconceptions.

Michael Bourton
Squadron Leader
Mess Historian
July 2003

Julia Trasler
Flight Lieutenant
Deputy Mess Historian
July 2003

Printed and bound by Stones the Printers Ltd.

Cover design by Adele Lilley
Published and designed by:
Lance Publishing Ltd
Grosvenor House, Eastgate, Whittlesey
Peterborough. PE7 1SE
Tel: 01733 751000

INDEX

	Page No.
Agents	.41
Agricultural Show Halton	.46
Animals	.21
Ante Room	.75
Appearance - Alfred	.15
Appearance - Gardens	.97
Art	.18
Attic - Bedrooms	.93
Bachelor's Quarters	.92
Bamfylde Room	.84
Basement - Service Wing	.55
Basement - Main House	.67
Bedding Table	.98
Bedrooms - Service Wing	.61
Belvedere	.37
Billiard Room	.82
Bothy	.103
Boucher Room	.87
Boudoir	.88
Bronzino Room	.82
Butler	.59
Cars	.61
Central Heating	.38
Chief Chauffeur	.61
Chief Cook	.60
Chimneys	.36
Circus	.100
Comments on House	.34
Communication - Alfred	.18
Construction - Interior	.37
Cricket Pavilion	.103
Dairy	.58
Dining Room	.84
Diplomacy - Alfred	.17
Early Life - Alfred	.15
Electricity	.39
Family Tree - Rothschilds	.14
Fire Service - Security	.64
Fountain	.99
Gardeners	.103
Garden features - existing	.98
Garden Entrance	.87
Gas	.39

	Page No.
Glass	.37
Grand Staircase	.71
Greenhouses	.98
Ground Floor - Main	.67
Ground Floor Plan - Service	.58
Gun Room	.83
Halton Manor	.27
Halton Village, 1900	.42
Halton Residents, 1900	.43
Head Coachman	.61
Health - Alfred	.22
Heirs - Alfred	.22
Housekeeper	.60
Kitchen Gardens	.98
Lake	.99
Laundry	.58
Lawrence Room	.78
Library	.85
Lily Langtry	.101
Lionel de Rothschild	.15
Main Entrance	.67
Main House Plan	.68
Mayer Amschel	.13
Mr de Rothschild's Room	.80
Music - Alfred	.20
Nathan Mayer	.14
North Drawing Room	.76
Paintings	.114
Personality - Alfred	.16
Plunge Bath.	.67
Police - Security	.65
Porch	.34
Present Use of Rooms	.112
Principal Bedrooms	.90
Properties - Rothschild	.25
Red Room	.80
Roof - Main House	.95
Roof - Service Wing	.61
Rooms - Basement	.55
Salon	.68
Sanitation	.39

	Page No.			Page No.
School - Village	.47			
Security	.64	Tenants		.46
Skittles Alley	.102	Theatre - Alfred		.21
Smoking Room	.81	Toilets - Basement		.57
South Drawing Room	.78	Transport - Alfred		.21
Special Gardens	.98			
Staff	.62	Water		.37
Steward	.58	Will		.118
Summer Houses	.103	Winter Gardens		.73
Swiss Chalet	.101	Work - Alfred		.16

BIBLIOGRAPHY AND REFERENCE MATERIAL

1830   Commercial Directory - Pigot

1847   History of Antiquities of the County of Buckinghamshire - Lipscombe

1864   The Gentleman's House - R. Kerr

1884   Works of Art in the Collection of A de Rothschild - C. Davis

1893   International Monetary Conference Memorandum, Minutes & Report

1908   Victoria County History

1919   Old Days in Bohemian London - Mrs C. Scott

1921   Ten Years at the Court of St James - Baron von Eckardstein

1922   Reminiscences - Lady Battersea

1925   Days I Knew - L. Langtry

1928   Rise of House of Rothschild - E. Corti
        Anglo-German Relationships in the First Decade of the Twentieth Century

1939   The Magnificent Rothschilds - C. Roth

1940   Flying Wild - C. Curzon

1942   Life's Ebb and Flow Countess of Warwick

1940s   Reading Lists - Lady de Rothschild

1955   Edwardians in Love - D. Leslie

1962   The Rothschilds - F. Morton

1964   Victoria RI - E. Longford

1970   The Edwardians - J.B. Priestley

1970   Foundation of the English Rothschilds - S.D. Chapman

1971   Halton House - G. Haydock

1973   Art Collections of A de Rothschild - N.D. de Rothschild

1973   The Rothschilds - V. Cowles

1975   Life in the English Country House - M. Girouard

1978   The Victorian Country House - M. Girouard

1980   The Rothschilds at Waddesdon Manor - Mrs J. de Rothschild

1981   Victorian and Edwardian Country House Life - Lambert

1981   The Gentleman's Country House and its Plan - J. Franklin

1982   Our Exbury - E. de Rothschild and A.J. Holland

NEWSPAPERS AND PERIODICALS

Bucks Herald

Burke's Peerage

Country Life

Dictionary of National Biography

Illustrated American

Jewish Chronicles

Kelly's Directories

The Times

Vanity Fair

Various Catalogues of Sale

WITH THANKS FOR HELP FROM THE FOLLOWING:

Aylesbury Public Library Local Collection

Air Historical Branch

Bath Museum of Costume

DOE/PSA

National Gallery

The Rothschild Archive Trust

The Royal Air Force Museum

Somerset House

Victoria and Albert Museum

Witt Library (Courtauld Institute)